SINISTER, STRANGE AND SUPERNATURAL

Anthologies by Helen Hoke

Ghostly, Grim and Gruesome
Eerie, Weird and Wicked
Terrors, Traumas and Torments
Thrillers, Chillers and Killers
A Chilling Collection

SINISTER, STRANGE AND SUPERNATURAL

An anthology by
HELEN HOKE

J.M. Dent & Sons Limited
London Toronto Melbourne

First published in Great Britain 1981
by J.M. Dent & Sons Ltd.

First published in the United States of America
by Elsevier/Nelson Books New York

Printed in the United States of American
for J.M. Dent & Sons Limited
Aldine House, Welbeck Street, London

British Library Cataloguing in Publication Data
Sinister, strange and supernatural.
1. Supernatural—Juvenile fiction
I. Hoke, Helen
823'.9'1J P25
ISBN 0-460-06072-4

Acknowledgments

The selections in this book are used by permission of and special arrangements with the proprietors of their respective copyrights, who are listed below. The editor's and publisher's thanks go to all who have made the collection possible.

The editor and publisher have made every effort to trace ownership of all material contained herein. It is their belief that the necessary permissions from publishers, authors, and authorized agents have been obtained in all cases. In the event of any questions arising as to the use of any material, the editor and publisher express regret for any error unconsciously made and will be pleased to make the necessary corrections in future editions of the book.

"Bookworm," by John Edgell. From *Ghosts* by John Edgell (Wayland Publishers).

"Contents of the Dead Man's Pocket," by Jack Finney. Copyright © 1956 by Jack Finney. Reprinted by permission of the Harold Matson Company, Inc.

ACKNOWLEDGMENTS

"Cool Air," by H. P. Lovecraft. Reprinted by permission of Arkham House Publishers, Inc., Sauk City, Wisconsin, from *The Dunwich Horrors and Others.*

"Forever and the Earth," by Ray Bradbury. Copyright 1950, by Ray Bradbury, renewed 1977. Reprinted by permission of the Harold Matson Company, Inc.

"Housebound," by R. Chetwynd-Hayes. By permission of the author. © R. Chetwynd-Hayes 1968.

"One Grave Too Few," by Lady Cynthia Asquith. From *The Second Ghost Book,* edited by Lady Cynthia Asquith, published by James Barrie Ltd. Reprinted by permission of the Hutchinson Publishing Group Ltd.

"The Pipe-Smoker," by Martin Armstrong. From *Selected Stories,* published by Jonathan Cape Ltd. Reprinted by permission of A. D. Peters & Co., Ltd.

"Transition," by Algernon Blackwood. Reprinted by kind permission of the Estate of Algernon Blackwood.

"The Walking Shadow," by Jean Stubbs. From *The Sixth Ghost Book,* 1970. Reprinted by permission of the Hutchinson Publishing Group Ltd.

"The Warlock," by Fritz Leiber. Copyright © 1959 by Great American Publications Inc. and reprinted by permission of E. J. Carnell Literary Agency.

Dedicated to Eirene Christodoúlou
in gratitude

Contents

About This Book 13

The Walking Shadow / *Jean Stubbs* 15

One Grave Too Few / *Cynthia Asquith* 31

Bookworm / *John Edgell* 52

Forever and the Earth / *Ray Bradbury* 63

Cool Air / *H.P. Lovecraft* 84

Transition / *Algernon Blackwood* 95

Housebound / *R. Chetwynd-Hayes* 103

Contents of the Dead Man's Pocket / *Jack Finney* 116

The Warlock / *Fritz Leiber* 137

The Pipe-Smoker / *Martin Armstrong* 150

SINISTER, STRANGE AND SUPERNATURAL

About This Book

The intent of all my anthologies is to intrigue, puzzle, perhaps delight readers, having made their nerves tingle first. This present collection, in particular, is not for the squeamish. As you read it through it, you will travel to several countries and go back a century or so in time—also to a science-fiction country that none of us has yet seen.

A thrilling variety of tales delving into murky scenes of macabre and sinister doings is the quintessence of this collection. The authors have been meticulously chosen for the masterly quality of their suspense writings.

According to that elegant and expert writer of the fantastic story, H. P. Lovecraft, a current of "Cool Air" can make one shiver, induce nausea—even revulsion. But let the author tell you why.

The breeze is chilly, as Tom Benecke, in "Contents of The

Dead Man's Pocket," stands perilously on a narrow window ledge eleven stories above a busy street in New York City—all because of an errant piece of paper.

In "Housebound," Celia Cooper is tempted to commit murder by necromancy—but meets instead a weird reversal of expectations.

John Mudbury, in the story "Transition," miraculously escapes danger in a city, only to land . . . where?

The story of a leading actor who will not stay dead is amusing and colorful. And if you are an admirer of Thomas Wolfe, you will be glad to think perhaps he is again writing—in another world, not yet reachable.

These brief references do not cover the entire contents. There is much more here equally sinister, strange, and supernatural—to guarantee chilly reading pleasure.

Helen Hoke

The Walking Shadow

JEAN STUBBS

Unlike most shades, this elegant spirit was seen on a grand scale in a dramatic setting.

Tom Beaumont died on his twelfth oyster, which was a bad one and cost the tavern a number of its customers in the next few months. The oyster was not entirely to blame. Add eleven others, and a pint and a half of white wine, to a corpulent gentleman in his late fifties who has lived too well. Join this to the excitement of a successful first night in a play by Mr. Wycherley. Throw in a tableful of good company, toasting stout Tom Beaumont as the greatest actor-manager in the city. And one faulty Whitstable oyster becomes the last step between this world and the next.

In the eighteenth century the church considered theatres to

be licensed dens of iniquity, and their players offshoots of the Devil, so there seemed to be no point in summoning the clergy while Tom gasped on the dirty floor of the tavern. But Sarah Beaumont—Tom's wife, and a fine actress, if somewhat overblown—found a drunken doctor, who finished off Tom's wine, bled him freely, and applied leeches in a lavish and haphazard fashion to his person. In spite of this treatment and several spoonfuls of Daffy's Elixir, Tom did not rally, but died with an actor-manager's philosophy on his lips.

"The theatre is all!" he whispered, and expired on the final syllable in great style: one splendid hand outflung, his Roman profile nobly turned to its best side.

He was buried in unconsecrated ground, which made Sarah cry, though Tom would not have cared twopence about it. Whether the church's censure made any difference to his state, or whether Tom would have refused to lie down in the holiest ground available, is not known. But he walked. It took him about a year to achieve his first appearance, and he made it a notable one. White's Theatre was crammed from roof to floor, and deep in conversation, when Tom Beaumont materialized before the curtain, bowing graciously. For a moment they took him to be the new manager, Ned Bellamy, and clapped encouragement. Then a gentleman of the Court leaned forward in his box and lifted his eyeglass. He took in the famous stance, one corpulent leg a little in advance of the other, one hand on the extravagantly ruffled cravat, the other behind the brocade coat. He recognized the florid countenance, the foppish wig, the vain little black eyes.

"Damme!" said the gentleman, aghast. "If it isn't Beaumont!"

The spirit seemed to possess his hearing, since he turned and bowed to the box in a gratified manner. The gentleman bowed back automatically, and Beaumont vanished, leaving chaos behind him. Unlike most shades he had been seen on a grand scale: not by one hysterical female on a dark night, nor by a frightened child in the grip of imagination, not by the simple, the gullible or the easily persuaded. Beaumont's ghost was viewed by an entire theatre audience, and the first act of *The Careless Husband* went for nothing.

Perhaps the restless dead, like the restless living, have a spiritual pilgrimage to make and must learn to conquer their personal vices before they can experience peace. Certainly Tom Beaumont resented his death, and resolved to harass the living as much as possible. He never forgave Sarah for marrying again, though he must have known that her generosity of body and heart made single life impossible. A buxom thirty-five, she gave her hand and a large share of White's Theatre to the new actor-manager, Ned Bellamy, less than a year after Tom's decease. By one of those inexplicable laws pertaining to ghosts, Tom was only allowed to haunt the theatre—perhaps because his own heart had been wholly there. So the new Mrs. Bellamy was able to enjoy her second husband's bed and company undisturbed at home. At the theatre she entered upon a series of incidents which were finally to drive her into retirement.

The first, beautifully timed, occurred one month after her remarriage, when she was gracing White's stage as Hamlet's mother. The closet scene had always been one of her best, but that evening she unwittingly surpassed herself. As Mr. Dishart, in the role of the Prince, reproached her in ringing tones, Sarah saw Tom Beaumont materialize beside him. It was a purely personal visitation, since Mr. Dishart gestured through Tom without noticing his presence, and the audience were disturbed by nothing stranger than Sarah's hysteria. She, horrified, put both hands over her mouth and began to walk backwards, whispering "No, no, no," into her tragedienne's black gloves. Mr. Dishart, inwardly cursing all actresses of consequence, attempted to follow her up. But Tom came with him, and Sarah retreated so piteously—and so very near to the wings—that Mr. Dishart stopped.

The admiration of the audience was tempered with some concern, as Hamlet—kept at a difficult distance—first repeated his cues, then hissed Sarah's lines, and finally carried on without her. And as he reviled the Queen for stewing in corruption, and making love over the nasty sty, Tom nodded belligerently. Reassured by the magnificent voice of Mr. Dishart, and Sarah's brilliant exhibition of terror and remorse, the spectators decided that Mr. Bellamy had improved on Mr. Shakespeare by cutting the Queen's speeches. Anxious to be in the vanguard of this latest innovation, they applauded so long and loudly that Sarah had to appear before them again and again, her eyes inflamed by smelling salts. In spite of idolatrous reviews she never dared play Queen Gertrude afterwards.

One by one, Tom plucked the laurel leaves from Sarah's good-natured brow. His campaign and her increasing flesh shortened her career. She made her last appearance on the English stage as Lady Macbeth.

Tom chose to reveal himself in the sleepwalking scene, and his timing was—as always—superb. As Sarah cried, "All the perfumes of Arabia will not sweeten this little hand!" he rose grinning at her side, saying, "Nor all the stays in the world lessen this vast girth! Madam, you have grown uncommonly fat!"

Forty years later, when other Lady Macbeths chilled the blood of their admirers, old men would say, "Why, sir, you should have seen *Mrs. Bellamy* in the sleepwalking scene. She groaned as if her heart was broke, I do assure you!"

Sarah lived until the age of seventy-five, secure and comfortable unless she set foot in White's Theatre. And Tom kept his resentment warm to the last, but he was cheated of her company. She died respectably, with a clear conscience and the blessing of the church, and never joined him.

With his wife off the boards, however, Tom turned his attention to Ned Bellamy, who was making a name for himself as a fine producer of Shakespearian tragedies. Now Shakespeare had a fondness for spectres, and gave them his maximum attention. Who could overlook Banquo's ghost at the feast, prevent a shiver as Caesar's helmeted shade strode the bloody battlefield at Phillipi, or ignore Hamlet's father's spirit in the opening scene of that play? Tom cast himself in these roles with a zest that approached ruthlessness. He even took the trouble to delay or temporarily disable the actor cast for the part, lest the necessary impact be lost.

Ned Bellamy was playing Brutus when Tom made his début towards the end of *Julius Caesar.* Stricken dumb with recognition, the audience were held captive while Ned Bellamy whispered, "Speak to me what thou art." Tom's powers were limited. He would have loved to boom out, "Thy evil spirit, Brutus," in that rich, hoarse voice with its overtones of good living. Instead he had to content himself with a ghostly glower, while Brutus swallowed and answered himself and carried on, somehow, without response. He had kept his head remarkably well, but long before he stammered that he would meet the shade at Phillipi a great rustle had passed through the house. Ladies were recovering their voices. They screamed, and fainted in silk heaps all over the theatre. And the men, white and silent, or red and swearing, leaped to their feet and put their hands to the hilts of useless swords. The players, professional even in this extremity, attempted to continue, but the noise was so great that Ned Bellamy ordered the curtain to be rung down, and no calls were taken.

The *London Morning Penny Post* gave a highly colored and inaccurate account of Beaumont's Ghost, and speculated on the reason for his appearance. The old rivalry between Bellamy and Beaumont was raked up, with unfavorable accounts of brawls in taverns and an abortive duel in Leicester Fields. There was a timely reminder that Mrs. Beaumont, as was, had become Mrs. Bellamy less than a year after her first husband's death. The writer headed his article, *"Et tu, Brute,"* which many people considered to be an exquisite summing up of the situation.

Tom was too busy studying his next part, as Hamlet's father's ghost, to be concerned with the refinements of the *London Morning Penny Post.* This time he stopped the play in the first act instead of the last. One soldier fell from the battlements and broke his leg. Bellamy, as Hamlet, suffered a mild heart attack and was abed for six weeks with ten leeches. And the spectators fled from the theatre.

Ned returned as Macbeth, resolved to sit Tom's persecution out. He had warned his company and the public that the late Mr. Beaumont might appear as Banquo's ghost, and to a certain degree they were prepared for this enormity. The attendance was excellent; and a Duchess, who should have been at home, almost produced the heir to a great estate in a White's Theatre box.

But Mr. Mills did very well as Banquo and his ghost, without Tom's aid, and the feast passed off as an anticlimax. What no one expected was a bravura display over the witches' cauldron. With a versatility truly amazing to behold, Tom impersonated an Armed Head, a Bloody Child, A Child Crowned with a Tree in his Hand, a Show of Eight Kings and—having previously tripped Mr. Mills up with a ghostly spear in the corridor—Banquo's ghost. More fascinated than afraid, the audience watched every move, and then burst into sincere applause. A spirit Tom certainly was, but it was the spirit of a great actor and a true professional, and they rose out of their seats to honor him. He disappeared on a bow, and the play proceeded in peace.

Ned Ballamy, shrewd and courageous, measured his haunter even as he spoke his final lines. He knew that Sarah, good-natured and indolent in her mantle of fat, did not possess the fibre to confront Tom. But he knew that he must conquer or appease him, or lose the theatre and his livelihood. Ned had not missed the sudden pleasure on that ghostly florid face when the spectators stood in his honor, and he respected the ingenuity that Tom had put into the performance. So, as they took curtain after curtain, and the Duchess was carried out groaning, Ned reached a conclusion. He walked forward to where the wicks floated in an iron trough and held out his arms for silence.

"We have been honored this evening by the presence of one well known to us," he said. "And therefore, my lords, ladies, and gentlemen, we shall leave the stage empty for a few moments, and I pray you give a token of your affection and esteem to the late great Mr. Thomas Beaumont."

Then he strode, heart beating too fast for his good or its own, into the wings. The audience, all fear exorcized, slapped and stamped and waved their handkerchiefs. The stage remained deserted by everything but three dusty benches—which represented the Plain before the Castle—and the shadows thrown by the gently swinging candelabra in the roof.

Then, very gradually, a stout gentleman with bright black eyes became visible, bowing and making a handsome leg. One hand spread affectedly across his lace cravat, the other wagged out of vanity behind his brocade coat. For fully a minute he accepted their plaudits. Then, just before he vanished, he looked directly at Ned Bellamy in a bewilderment of anger and gratitude. And Ned bowed very deeply and gravely and said, "Your servant, sir!"

His sting drawn, as it were, Tom became a part-time member of the company. Ned let it be known that, though there was no guarantee, the late Mr. Beaumont might well appear—either as himself or someone else—at any time. And his virtuoso performance in *Richard III* was long remembered, when he appeared in quick succession as the ghosts of Prince Edward, King Henry the Sixth, Clarence, Rivers, Grey and Vaughan, Hastings, the two young Princes, Lady Anne, and Buckingham—enough to disturb the sleep of any monarch. Sometimes he was observed standing a little shyly on the edge of the company, in a play which could not absorb his peculiar talents, and then Ned kindly summoned everyone from the stage, and the audience gave Tom Beaumont a special hand. And White's Theatre entered upon a decade of popularity, which was later attributed by historians to the quality of management, since they could hardly subscribe to the drawing power of a ghost.

Fire demolished White's in the latter part of the eighteenth century. Ned Bellamy died of a heart attack, attempting to fight flames beyond any man's control—even when that man is a desperate lover, resolved to rescue his lady. Gossip and malicious rumor said that Tom Beaumont started the fire in one of the tiring rooms, and was seen laughing in the ruins as his rival died. The *London Morning Penny Post* embroidered this story to such an extent that *The Gentleman's Magazine* felt bound to contradict it. There were witnesses to the event, they said, who saw Mr. Beaumont appear at Mr. Bellamy's side and attempt to pick up the bucket that fell from his hand. And many persons had seen him sitting in the ruins, like some masculine Niobe, weeping for his double loss.

Tom was lonely when Ned went, and vexed when Sarah followed him. And as the new theatre façade went up, and a new manager founded a new company, Tom discovered himself cherishing even such slight acquaintances as Mr. Mills; simply because he had tripped him up with a ghostly spear, and borrowed his part for a few minutes. The new White's Theatre was grander and less lovable than the old one. An air of fighting gloriously against all odds had gone with the fire. White's was established now, prosperous, and far less exciting.

The new century, too, seemed to have sacrificed grace for bustle. As the Industrial Revolution became a reality instead of a threat, as the industrious Victorians replaced the elegant Georgians, Tom became a displaced ghost. He sulked at his changed world, and pondered his exclusive position, for no one joined him. He had thought they would form a ghostly company, and continue in death as in life—only minus the inconveniences of life. But one by one his friends and colleagues left him; and when the humdrum soul of Mr. Mills twanged straight to its Maker, Tom wept.

He had not the heart, if such an expression is permitted, to make a public appearance before 1840. By accident, he chose to materialize in the royal box when Her Majesty Queen Victoria was enjoying an evening at White's. Fortunately she was not disturbed, since two ushers attempted to turn him quietly out—and Tom, unused to such treatment, vanished in a huff. Later, glowering around a corner, he overheard them talking.

"It wasn't real, my dear fellow. My hand went straight through its shoulder. Have they got a ghost here, do you imagine?"

The usher was very young, no great lover of the theatre proper, and no historian.

"It couldn't have been anyone of consequence," he said, "or I should have recognized him."

Blighted, Tom sat alone in the empty theatre for a long time. He had thought that this life-in-death, monotonous though it often was, would go on unchanged for ever. But nothing remains the same, even for a walking shadow, and Tom Beaumont, as actor, manager, and ghost, was forgotten.

The theatre, once a dream of white and gold, was painted gaudily in the second half of the nineteenth century, christened White's Follies and given over to Music Hall capers. Tom had no experience of this new medium, and no opportunity—since his haunting was limited—of comparing one Music Hall with another. But he recognized the second-rate when he saw it, and his pride suffered. In one or two of the players he felt there was something like promise, and when the audiences felt the same he was relieved and flattered. But he also noticed that if an actor or actress reached a certain standard of excellence they disappeared elsewhere, leaving him to contemplate performing dogs, and comedians with red noses.

A second fire, at which Tom did not assist with the water buckets, ravaged White's Follies. He stood there gravely, hands behind his brocade coat, wig set aright, and contemplated the blaze with infinite satisfaction. Since he could not have his old building, he preferred rubble. Spirits, as well as human beings, have their miseries and glories. The great difference is the time factor. So most of the nineteenth century had passed as wretchedly for Tom as, say, a decade would have dragged along in true life. He had grown accustomed to being ignored and unknown. He had survived the loss of his era and his contemporaries and the threatre as he once knew it. And he had learned to wait, to be passive. So he raised himself quite jauntily on his heels, and craned his neck to observe a great beam crumble and fall in a shower of sparks. He was extremely interested in the new fire-fighting contraptions: the scarlet and brass monster, bell ringing, hurtling through the streets; the men in strange uniforms and shining helmets; the yards of rubber hose and jets of water. It was the best evening he had had in the last fifty years. If only he had been able, a lady on each arm, to celebrate the event at a tavern afterwards—the oysters, the wine, the company—

A group of City gentlemen, rich in pocket and reverent of theatre history, rebuilt White's under its former name. A new management attempted to devote itself to the presentation of Restoration Drama. They found it expedient, however, to intersperse this with popular comedy; and at last specialized in light fare, with an occasional Restoration piece thrown in for good measure.

Tom, ever adaptable, took part when he could. But a ghost, generally speaking, is as noticeable as his audience makes him; and Tom was either overlooked or accepted as a genuine member of the crowd scenes. The 1920's were upon him, and down he went in a flood of cigarette-holders, long beads, short skirts, and general scepticism. Sullenly, he walked through scenery to keep in practice. Unnoticed, he appeared in dressing-rooms, to be put down as an excess of lobster or alcohol. Pettishly, he soon refused to materialize at all—and was never missed.

In the thirties the threatre was converted into a cinema, around which he wandered in total bewilderment. A shadow himself, he could not understand the shadows on the screen. Real from a distance, they became unsubstantial at close range. He must have vanished through the glowing screen a thousand times in an effort to find them. But what changes of character, costume and country! What landscapes and seascapes, what drawing-room scenes, what minute detail! He marveled at the ingenuity, walked closer to touch or inspect some specially fine article of furniture or china—and found nothing. Later, he stood behind the projector and watched the operator spin his reels of magic. And when the lights were out and the house empty he sat for hours, contemplating this new phenomenon. Then he rose and sighed, brushed imaginary dust from his breeches and set his wig aright, and said aloud, "Damme! What a princely spectacle I should have made of *Macbeth* with this moving theatre. Why, sir," though no companion was there to hear him, "I could have put on a battle scene such as would have had the ladies in a faint, and the gentlemen reaching for their swords."

In time he became a connoisseur of this new medium; separating the good from the indifferent, and nourishing a particular fondness for Marlene Dietrich. He later added Rita Hayworth and Marilyn Monroe to his list of favorites.

The cinema queues waned, drawn away by yet another innovation of which Tom was ignorant—the television. He had not been a manager, alive or dead, for two centuries, without sensing financial disaster. In sorrow he counted the empty seats, and clicked his tongue and shook his head. Unsurprised, he watched the programmes become desperately popular without effect. And when the doors finally closed, he mourned this latest passing.

Decorators arrived, sharpening his interest briefly, but they brought no glad tidings. The cinema became a Bingo Hall. It took Tom only three weeks to decide that this was not his métier, and then he acted. His appearance from the shadows, foppishly dressed and with one wrathful arm extended, caused great consternation. And lest anyone should think they had been mistaken he appeared nightly, in the same place and in the same attitude. The Hall was shut at the end of his first week's performance—for repairs, the management said. Tom knew better, and slapped his thighs and laughed until his shoulders and belly shook. Then he waited for the next move.

It came in the homely shape of a medium, whom the manager escorted to the theatre the following Sunday, in a mixture of urgency and embarrassment.

Tom surveyed her with contemptuous interest, being a sexual snob; and wondered afresh why any woman chose to live after losing her physical attractions. But Mrs. Rout had interests other than the pleasure of the opposite sex, and snuffed the air in much the same fashion as a retriever snuffs game.

"There's something here," she announced, rubbing her hands and smiling. "Oh, my word, yes! Very strong. Very strong. You did well to call me in."

Then she requested absolute silence, sat down with her hands pressed over her eyes, and concentrated. For the first time in two hundred years or so, Tom was aware of communication, though no word was spoken. And he stood up, brought to judgment. But his first words were as arrogant as ever.

"Madam," he said. "I should be monstrous obliged if you would take your leave of me!"

"I want to help you," purred Mrs. Rout, intent upon her own purposes. "I can give you peace and rest."

"Madam," said Tom irritably, "I have had enough rest to content any man living or dead—and I never asked for peace. But, madam, if you have any influence with the present management, I do beg you to impart this message. Tell them, if you please, that I shall continue to appear nightly until some form of genuine theatre returns to this unhappy building!"

The medium moaned and held her neck.

"Ah. You have had a constriction here," she cried. "I feel it. You died of a constriction." Her imagination leaped ahead of her. "Choking, choking. Now I see it all. You hanged yourself in a dressing-room—the aura was very strong there when I came in."

"Pox on you, madam," said Tom rudely. "I died of a rotten oyster!"

"Should we fetch a clergyman, Mrs. Rout?" the manager whispered. "And then the poor—soul—could be exorcized."

"God's teeth, sir," cried Tom. "No clergyman shall meddle with me, alive or dead!"

"Poor wandering spirit," said Mrs. Rout, absorbed in her own misguided sympathy. "You shall have *rest.* You *shall* have rest."

In vain Tom swore at her, shook her shoulder, kicked the manager, and shouted imprecations at the top of his ghostly voice. The medium suddenly came to, sneezed, smiled, reached for her handbag, and requested to be taken forthwith back to Balham.

On Tuesday night the exorcism took place, with a discretion and thoroughness truly admirable. In a matter of minutes Tom felt as though his feet had been untethered. He bobbed up to the ceiling, in a positive fusillade of oaths, and soared out into the evening sky—leaving those below to congratulate themselves and him on his freedom.

In rage and terror he floated over London, catching at chimney pots and spires, at weathercocks and steeples, until an arm as insubstantial as his own arrested him.

"Ned Bellamy!" said Tom, amazed. And then sternly, to cover his delight, he cried: "Well, sir, you have been long enough looking up an old acquaintance!"

"Why, Tom, the fault is of your own making. You *would* stay, sir."

Tom took a slow turn around St. Paul's dome and came to rest, clinging to Ned's ruffles.

"*I* would stay, sir?" he cried indignantly.

"Aye, sir, and *shall* stay if you wish. Though I promise you we are all very well in another place."

"Have I a choice, then, Ned?" Tom asked.

The nod astonished him, and his brows contracted as he thought.

"Ned," he said wistfully. "I should like to stay just a while longer, Ned! Do not go for a moment, I pray you! I am like a damned pigeon wheeling when you take away your arm. I am not yet used to the motion. Ned, I have all manner of things to tell you. They have moving theatres, Ned, that live in round boxes and are shone onto a screen. And the players now are something different from our own."

"Vanity, Tom, all vanity. I could tell you of things so fine that you could never imagine them. Vanity, Tom."

The little black eyes twinkled. One splendid hand brushed a speck of ghostly dust from the ghostly cravat.

"Ah, but Ned," said Tom shyly, "I was always a vain man! A little while longer, Ned. A mere century or so. What difference can that make to my eternity? Just to see, Ned. Just to watch.

But you will ask me again?" he added, with some anxiety.

"Aye, Tom. Go your ways! And take care while you find your legs again. These steeples are the very devil for a middle-aged ghost on a dark night!"

Like one released from prison, Tom Beaumont floated and peered and pondered. Unrestricted by White's Theatre, he was seeking employment, and had all the leisure in the world with which to find it.

There is a new traveling theatre company in the United States of America, who specialize in Shakespearian plays. At first they had a hard, thin time of it, but their fame is growing and they expect to tour Europe this winter. The company does not encourage the questions and attention of the Press, which gives them the finest publicity available because of this peculiar reticence.

They have their idiosyncrasies, such as producing all their plays in eighteenth-century costume. But their particular genius lies in illusion and effect. I think that of all their productions I would recommend *Macbeth.* The spectacle over the witches' cauldron is truly astonishing for its versatility. Though I *have* heard critics express a preference for *Richard III,* when no less than eleven ghosts in quick succession chill the blood, and send a murmur of admiration and terror through the house. And I must admit that I have never seen Hamlet's father's ghost so well portrayed; while the sight of Caesar's helmeted shade, striding the bloody battlefield at Phillipi, would bring a clutch of horror to the stoutest heart.

One Grave Too Few

CYNTHIA ASQUITH

"Sacred to the memory of Grizel Cramp 1770–1850," read one of the gravestones in the small churchyard of Greystock Manor.

"Do you believe in ghosts?" I had the temerity to ask the very distinguished old man who had devoted most of his life to psychical research. Touched, I think, by my extreme youth and eagerness, he was courteous enough to answer my crude question seriously.

"It depends, my dear girl, what you *mean* by ghosts," he said in his mournful, resonant voice. "I don't believe that spirits of the dead return to earth to haunt the living. No, I don't believe in *spectres*. But I do believe in that kind of haunting which is caused by a perpetuation of the past. That's to say, I think—in fact, I know—a house can be haunted because of its having once been the scene of some experience so intense that a record of that experience has stayed on the air. Thus, certain sounds and sights, first heard, first seen long, long ago, may still be transmitted to the eyes and ears of living persons. Not, of course, to everyone's.

"One person may be quite impervious to this—how shall I put it?—this presence of the past; another so susceptible that she may come almost to identify herself with whosoever it was whose anguish still vibrates on the air. Should that terrible experience—be it pain, grief, or terror—happen to be transmitted at a time when for some reason, such as any exceptional strain, the veil of the flesh, which is our screen, is out of repair, then the effect on the nervous system may be very serious. A fatal shock can even be given."

"Do you think you yourself have ever actually come across such a case?" I ventured to ask.

"Yes, I do," he answered gravely. "At all events, I knew one man so convinced of such a fatality that he had what was perhaps the loveliest small Manor House in England razed to the ground."

I begged the speaker to tell me what had driven a man to destroy his own home. Gradually yielding to my entreaties, he gave me all the "evidence"—that was what he called it—collected, he explained, from various witnesses. The broken-hearted young owner of the house had told all he could bring himself to tell, and two doctors, the nurse, the vicar and several villagers had all been cross-examined.

It is twenty years ago since I listened to that composite story, the various threads of which I have woven into one consecutive narrative. Here it is:

It was in May 1910 that John and Laura Bryan first came to live in the house they had bought shortly after their marriage some ten months before. Both of them had fallen in love at first sight with Greystock Manor. The house had been unoccupied for a good many years, but Laura's heart was so set on their first child being born in its future home that she insisted on scrambling in as soon as just a few rooms were ready. The much that remained to be done could wait until she was up and around again, when they would all three go away for a while and leave the workmen to finish. The house agent had told the Bryans that the Thorne family—the original owners of the house—had died out over a hundred years ago. Beyond this one fact, the new owners knew nothing whatever of the house's history. Nor did they care. Its future and their plans for its beautification were all that concerned them.

Laura was enchanted by the long, low, white-panelled bedroom with its tall carved chimney-piece and great bow window overlooking the paved courtyard, and across that on to the wide lawns stretching down to the silver thread of the river far below. Excitedly she pointed out the exact place where she must, so she told John, have a sunken garden. This time next year it would be filled with grape hyacinths. As she opened the mullioned window she caught sight of some writing scratched on the glass of one of its leaded panes. "Prudence Prew 1840," she read out. "What a pretty name! 1840. Seventy years ago! Prudence Prew . . . ? I wonder who and what she was. I hope she was happy in my room. What do you suppose Prudence was like, John?"

John said she must have been very tall to be able to write her name so high up on the window.

"Poor Prudence Prew, how tall she grew!" improvised Laura.

As soon as every tangled twist and turn of the long-neglected garden had been explored, Laura declared they must go and have a good look at the churchyard. She could see, she said, that Greystock would be just as lovely a place to be dead in as to live in. They would choose the exact spot where they would be buried. She spoke as speak those too young, too happy, really to believe in death.

Many of the departed Thornes lay buried in the shade of the dark yew trees whose twisted old trunks looked as though for centuries they had striven to writhe their roots out of the earth. Except for the imposing monuments to that one family, the small churchyard was for the most part crowded only with the simplest graves—some mere nameless mounds of grass; others plain slabs of stone either lying flat, or standing aslant at odd angles. John and Laura smiled over some of the inscriptions which set forth the many virtues of those who "Not Lost, But Gone Before" had either "Fallen Asleep" or else "Gone to Rest." No one had simply died. When they came to one pitifully small grass mound, Laura stood still. She was in the tremulous state of happiness when the eyes easily brim with tears, and her voice faltered as she read out the inscription cut on a roughly hewn piece of plain wood:

I had a dove, and the sweet dove died.

"That's the only *child's* grave I can see," said John.

"Most of the rude forefathers seem to have lived to a ripe old age. Look at this one! 'Here Lies Matthew Mudd'—what a good name!—'who fell asleep in the 99th year of his life. And also, Martha, his wife, who followed him to rest aged 92.' "

Laura hurried from grave to grave. "I can't find poor Prudence Prew anywhere, can you, John?" she asked.

"Prudence was probably a spinster of this parish. I expect she married and lived happily ever afterwards."

"I hope so," said Laura. "Oh, look, John! Here's another good name. 'Sacred to the memory of Grizel Cramp 1770–

1850. For forty years midwife of Greystock Parish. Suffer the little children to come unto Me.' "

The Bryans chuckled over the well-chosen text.

"Old Grizel Cramp, The Village Gamp," laughed Laura with what she referred to as her bad habit of improvising doggerel couplets. "Poor old Grizel! I must say I'm rather thankful I shan't have to depend on her ministrations."

The mossed weathered old stones merged so well into the quiet green of the graveyard that John and Laura loudly deplored two solitary exceptions that stood out in glaring white.

"Let's see who perpetrated this atrocity," said Laura, approaching a frightful alabaster angel with harp, palm, and heavenward-pointing forefinger.

Sacred to the memory of Lilian, dearly beloved wife of Henry Still of Greystock Manor 1877–1899.

"Oh dear!" exclaimed Laura. "Only twenty-two! I wonder why she died so young."

They walked up to the other monstrous white monument, an over-life-size figure of The Reaper, complete with scythe and hour-glass.

To the memory of Rachel, dearly beloved wife of James Gowan 1878–1903. Born to know not Winter, only Spring.

"Poor Rachel!" sighed Laura. "I wonder where *she* lived—and died."

"Probably at the Vicarage," said John. "No cottager could have misspent so much money, and there aren't any other houses in the parish."

"But it doesn't put the *Reverend* James Gowan," objected Laura.

They turned away and hand in hand retraced their steps down the long yew-tree walk. Laura declared she must tell the gardener about her sunken garden at once. John said he wasn't sure he liked sunken gardens. Why was she so set on one? Her answer was conclusive. There had been a sunken garden in her childhood's home and no babyhood must be without the special enchantment this had held for her.

Life was radiant to John and Laura—few ever know such happiness; none more than once—but never again after this first golden evening in their new home was their happiness quite unclouded. Laura, rapturous, but tired after her long journey and the excitement of the arrival, went early to bed. Alas, the lovely bedroom she had so long looked forward to brought disappointment. She, as a rule so sound, so dreamless a sleeper, had the first really bad night of her life.

John was distressed next day by the dark blue shadows under her eyes. Her expression, too, was rather troubled. She seemed preoccupied; even—and he had never known her thus—depressed. Questioned, she admitted to not feeling "quite herself." It wasn't so much the staying awake she minded, but when at last she did fall asleep, she'd had such a horrid dream. She wouldn't say what she had dreamed. "Mere nonsense," she declared it to be; yet, it seemed to John that even by the end of the day she hadn't quite shaken off the effect of that dream, and at night, climbing rather wearily into bed, she said with a sigh, "I think this is quite the most beautiful room I've ever seen, but I'm not sure that it's a *happy* room."

It must have been about a week later that the vicar came to luncheon for the first time. An amiable, spinsterish little man, he evidently took great personal pride in his beautiful church and what he called its "quaint" graveyard. Delighted by the Bryans' appreciation and anxious to display the sense of humor on which he also prided himself, he cackled when Laura told him how much the text chosen for the village Gamp had amused her. Grizel Cramp, he declared, had grown to be quite a "legendary figure," and the village still boasted one "aged crone" old enough to remember her—Martha Mudd, the daughter-in-law of the old sexton Matthew Mudd.

Laura asked the vicar if he could tell her anything about a Prudence Prew whose name was scratched on a window-pane in the house. He said he had been told some people called Prew had once owned the Manor House, but only for a very short time. John denounced the two incongruous alabaster monuments. The vicar agreed they were A Great Pity.

"Why did that poor lady of the house—Lillian Still I think her name was—die so young?" asked Laura.

"I really couldn't say, Mrs. Bryan. The Stills were before my time. I've only had this living for two years," replied the vicar. "What very lovely weather we are enjoying for the time of year, are we not?"

"Who put up that other white horror—the one with the reaper and the scythe?" asked Laura.

"I don't know," answered the vicar, seemingly absorbed in rolling his bread into gray pills as tiny as he could possibly make them.

John felt sure the phrase "I really couldn't say" had been the vicar's way of avoiding a direct lie, and once Laura had gone upstairs to rest it did not take much pressure to break down the guest's feeble defences.

"It's no good, Mr. Bryan," twittered the vicar, "it's no good whatever my trying to keep back facts, which of course anyone in the village would be only too willing to supply. Since you ask, I must confess that, though of course the matter is one of mere—the merest—coincidence, I do admit that under the present—er—happy circumstances—I did prefer not to tell your charming lady that the second unfortunate young woman who was—er—taken so young—the one whom she inquired about—had also—er—died in this house."

"What did they die of?" asked John.

The little vicar looked miserable.

"Well," he bleated. "As a matter of fact—again, as I say, the merest coincidence—actually both—er—yes, both of them died in—er—childbirth. Too sad! Too sad! So unusual nowadays. But, of course, you won't let such a mere coincidence trouble you, will you, Mr. Bryan?"

"Of course not. Why ever should it?" John said robustly and changed the subject.

As soon as the vicar left, John went up to see Laura. He found her lying fast asleep on the bed. Seldom had he seen her look so lovely—never quite so touchingly young. Thank goodness she was not what some called "fanciful." Nevertheless she must not hear of that strange "coincidence." How many women died in that way nowadays? A minute percentage! Had he ever personally known one who had? Not so far as he could remember. He must take great care no village gossip got at Laura.

She looked so tired next day that John decided to send for the doctor; and as he was coming he might just as well, as a matter of mere curiosity—so John told himself—be questioned about those two unfortunate cases. The doctor found nothing wrong with Laura, but prescribed a sedative. Intercepting him on his way out of the house, John plunged straight into the matter. "Of course that kind of thing meant nothing to him," he assured the doctor, but with women you never knew, so he hoped his wife wouldn't come to hear of those two young women who had so recently, and within only four years of one another, died in this house. By the way, could the doctor tell him why they had died? What had gone wrong?

The doctor said neither of the two women had been his patients. He had taken up this practice only five years ago. Pressed, he gave John, with obvious reluctance, the name of his predecessor, and his present address, some fifty miles away.

John didn't find his letter to the unknown doctor easy to write, nor did it receive a satisfactory reply—merely the bare statement that Dr. Browne was unable to give any information regarding the death of Mrs. Still, which had occurred before his time. Mrs. Gowan had died in giving birth to a child. John telephoned for an appointment.

The doctor made no pretence of being glad to see his visitor. John said he trusted he was not asking for any breach of medical etiquette, but as his wife was expecting a baby in about two months and he was afraid some village gossip might reach her ears, in which case she would quite likely ask awkward questions, would Dr. Browne mind being asked why Mrs. Gowan had died? Had she suffered from some particular weakness?

"No," answered the doctor. "As far as I could discover, there was nothing wrong with the poor young lady. As a matter of fact she died of heart failure."

"I see," said John. "I suppose she had a weak heart."

"If she had, it was the worst miss of my life," the doctor answered curtly. "Her heart seemed to me—and, of course, I examined it thoroughly—perfectly sound."

"Queer, wasn't it?" asked John.

"As you press me, Mr. Bryan, I can only say that, according to my diagnosis, the patient died of shock, but *why* she should have died of shock, I confess I have no idea whatever."

John said he supposed that to a nervous woman the mere fact of having a first baby was in itself a shock.

"It *wasn't* her first baby," said the doctor. "She'd had one two years before and been as right as rain. And, as I've said, the second occasion was a perfectly normal delivery. No, it was just one of those baffling cases."

"Do you know anything about the other young woman who died in the house four years before?"

"I was afraid you'd ask me that. Naturally there was talk in the village, and I did take steps to get into touch with the doctor who had attended her. The queer thing was that in that case, too, there had been no—er—*medical* reason for the unfortunate young woman's death. In fact the late Dr. Field—between ourselves, he was a queer nervy sort of chap—used a very unprofessional term. He said his patient had died of fright."

"Of *fright?*"

"I've no idea what he meant. Unless it was just that it was *her* first baby, and possibly she was an exceptionally nervous woman."

John remained silent.

The doctor suddenly expanded. "Look here, Mr. Bryan," he said in a much more sympathetic tone. "You and I are sensible people. We know that the fact of these two sad deaths having occurred in the same house is just a sheer fluke. What *else* could it be? Nevertheless, there's no denying the effect of auto-suggestion. So for fear of the peculiar circumstances coming to your wife's ears—no place like a small village for gossip—don't you think it would be advisable for her to change her room? I take it she does occupy the large front room with the bow window?"

John thanked Dr. Browne for his advice and hurried home.

Distressed to see traces of tears on Laura's face, he asked why she had been crying. There was nothing the matter she declared. It was just that several bad nights in succession were making her feel tired.

Had she had another bad dream? Under John's insistent

questioning, she admitted to having several times dreamed very much the same dream as the one which had upset her the first night. But what that dream was she wouldn't tell. Please, he mustn't ask her. No, he would think her too silly. John took this opportunity to suggest a change of bedroom. This she declared to be quite out of the question. Neither of the only other two possible bedrooms was anywhere near ready. The rain came through the ceiling in one; the floor of the other needed repairing.

When Laura had gone upstairs for her afternoon rest, John set off for a walk. As he came out of the wrought-iron gate, he found just outside it a very old bent woman, who was peering through a gap in the great yew hedge which enclosed the garden. At sight of him she became greatly excited. Brushing aside the wisps of white hair that fell over her bleared eyes, she stared searchingly into his face. Then, pointing with a palsied hand at his house, she broke into incoherent gabblings. John assumed her wits to be partly gone. In any case he could at first make out very little of her toothless mumbles. But it was obvious that she was trying very hard to tell him something.

"Grizel Cramp. Grizel Cramp," he heard her repeat several times.

For some time those names were the only two words he caught, but gradually snatches of speech became audible: "I tells old Grizel Cramp. Yes, I tells her. I did. . . . Poor girl! . . . I couldn't never forget her. Fair shrieked out, she did. I can hear her now! . . . 'Help! Help! Fetch Grizel! Fetch Grizel!' Lovely girl she was, and hadn't meant no harm, I'm sure, bless her innocent face. Been taken advantage of, I'll be bound. You take care, Sir, of your young lady, bless her. A sight for sore eyes she be. But this isn't no place for her; not as she be now. You mark my words, Sir. Best take her away quick."

The old woman clutched hold of John's arm. She pointed to the churchyard, and with one finger to her lips whispered, "One grave too few. Yes, yes. *One grave too few.*"

John did not know how to disengage himself from the old woman, and he was afraid that, left to herself, she would make her way into the garden. He felt sure she was bent on finding Laura. That mustn't be. It was a relief when the vicar appeared.

"Now then, Tibby. What are you doing here?" asked the vicar. "You know you aren't allowed out by yourself."

Taking hold of the old creature's skinny arm he led her to a small nearby cottage.

"You shouldn't let your old Granny wander off by herself, Miss Mudd," he said to the middle-aged woman who came to the door.

"I assume that was the 'aged crone' of whom you told us, vicar," said John as the two men walked away together.

"Yes, that's old Tibby Mudd."

"I couldn't hear all she said, but she did say a lot about Grizel Cramp, and she seemed to have something very much on her mind."

"Her *mind*?" echoed the vicar. "I don't think there's much left of that! But I believe I have heard she used to have some bee in her bonnet about the old midwife."

If the vicar knew what that bee was, he evidently had no intention of divulging it. Nor did John persist. He had already decided the old woman's granddaughter would be much easier to "get things out of." So next day, on the pretext of taking old Tibby a present of fruit, he called at the cottage, and when Miss Mudd told him her grandmother was upstairs in bed, he said he would be very obliged if she could throw any light on whatever it might be her old grandmother had seemed so anxious to tell him. Miss Mudd said she was sure she "didn't rightly know whether she did ought to tell." However, it didn't take long to break down her discretion. She became volubly forthcoming. This was the gist of what she called "Granny's story."

"Granny was the only one left alive as could still remember old Grizel Cramp—her as had been midwife so long. Ever so many babies she had brought into the world, but Granny, she always says as there had been one time when Grizel did ought to have been sent for, but hadn't never been fetched. . . . It didn't do to take much notice of what old folks said, but as you asked me, Sir, that's what Granny says. She says, too, as her old man—that's my grandfather—him as was sexton here for forty years, had been done out of one grave as he did ought to have dug. Yes, Sir, Granny was always saying as how there was one grave too few in the old churchyard.

"I'm not saying there's anything in it, Sir, mark you, but this was what Granny had got into her head and nothing couldn't get it out. It was way back when she was naught but a young girl that some folks called Prew come to live up at the Manor. They wasn't there more than two year. Just a man and his wife with the one daughter. Harsh, stern folks they was, Granny says—yes, proper Puritanical folk. They had but the one child, a young daughter, and Granny says as everyone wondered how a father and mother like they was could have come by such a daughter. Beautifullest girl she ever saw, Granny says she was, and that tall! She never did see another young lady so tall. They kept themselves to themselves, did the Prews. No one didn't hardly know them. And the maids wasn't scarcely ever allowed out. One late summer the maids all left—the gardeners too—and it was put about the village that the young lady—Miss Prudence her name was—had some illness as was very infectious, so everyone had been sent away so they shouldn't take it. But no doctor wasn't never fetched.

"Then one day my Granny's tom kitten gets lost, so she ventures through the gate into the garden up at the Manor to see had it strayed there, and as she was looking for Pussy, the door of the house bursts open, and the tall girl—Miss Prudence Prew as was—Granny sees her slip out of the house, like as though there was someone after her. Terrible scared she look.

"White as a sheet her face was, and she was crying fit to break your heart. You never did see anyone in such a state, Granny says. Then Granny sees Mrs. Prew's face look out of a window above, and when she catches sight of her daughter below a-trying to get away, she fair shakes her fist at her. The next moment she and her husband comes running out of the door, and they catches hold of their daughter and drags her back into the house. Granny says her struggles and her cries and the way she wrung her poor hands was pitiful. There wasn't no ring on her left hand, poor girl, but Granny says there did ought to have been; for Grizel Cramp was wanted. Yes, anyone could see that—plain as plain it was. That set Granny thinking, and she called to mind a handsome young gentleman—a 'mud student' they names him—that had been and gone in the summer, and then she remembers as how one day she'd seen him and Miss Prudence coming out of the wood together.

"And, of course, mind you, them Prews was the kind of folk that would stop at nothing rather than have shame come to the family. Granny tells her mother what she seen, but her mother says she's not to talk silly, nor poke her nose into what wasn't her business.

"After that, Granny often looks into that garden as was always kept fast locked, but she don't see nothing more, not for some weeks. Then one evening she makes so bold as to climb over the iron gate, slip inside and hide behind of a tree as was quite near to the house. She done this many a time. And one evening as she stands there, she sees poor Miss Prudence staring out at one of the windows. All pale and twisted her face was—wild-like. And when she sees Granny she opens the window and calls out 'Help me! Oh, help me! Help! Help! Fetch Grizel, fetch Grizel!' But her father and her mother appears at the window behind of her, and they catches hold of her and drags her back away from the window. Then the mother, with her cruel hard face, she pulls the curtains sharp to, and Granny couldn't see no more.

"Granny was set on telling Grizel how she'd heard her hollered for, but that evening she comes out in a rash, and her mother puts her to bed with the measles. Proper ill she was, and when she gets well again she hears as how, a few days after she was took ill, the Prews had driven away in a hired carriage, and hadn't never come back. They'd driven away with the blinds of the carriage drawn right down so that nobody couldn't see them go. It got about the village as poor Miss Prudence's illness had misfigured her, so they didn't want no one to see her. But Granny always says that, sure as sure, it wasn't more than *two* persons as drove away in that carriage.

"The house had been sold to that Mr. Still whose young wife was took. Ever so sad that was! Then the poor widowed gentleman, he sold the house to the Gowans, and she was took too, and then the house had stood empty for seven years."

John thanked Miss Mudd for telling him the story, but told her he thought her grandmother must have dreamed the whole thing.

When he called on his way home at the doctor's house to consult him about Laura's bad nights, he mentioned that he had just been told an extraordinary story about his new home. The doctor said he knew there was some old wife's tale about the Manor, but that he never paid any attention to such things.

Nevertheless in his opinion it was most important that Mrs. Bryan, whose nerves undoubtedly were upset, shouldn't hear any unpleasant village talk. That being so, it wasn't really safe ever to let her go out of the house by herself.

"So, Mr. Bryan," said the doctor, "as business takes you away from time to time, I have a suggestion to make. I happen to know that the excellent nurse, engaged to come in six weeks, is free now. Why not let her come at once and keep an eye on your wife?"

John agreed with alacrity. He was nervous as to how Laura might take this plan, but she raised no objection whatever. In fact—it struck him with a pang—she looked relieved.

John and Laura both took to the nurse at first sight. They liked her sensible, sensitive face, and quiet voice. "How blessedly unlike my picture of Grizel Cramp!" exclaimed Laura.

The nurse expatiated on the beauty of the house—"So full of atmosphere," she declared it to be, adding, "but then, of course I'm terribly psychic."

Hitherto this usually complacent statement had invariably made John writhe with boredom, but the nurse said it so unselfconsciously that he merely smiled.

Two days after the nurse's arrival, business took John up to London for a night. On his return he was pleased to see, as he drove up to the house, that at last the obstinate old gardener had started to dig Laura's sunken garden—a job put off again and again on pretext of the unfavorable condition, either of the ground or of his own lumbago.

The nurse met John in the hall. Could she have a word with him? She was afraid he would think her very silly, but, being psychic, she knew how very important the atmosphere of a patient's room was, and try as she would, she couldn't like Mrs. Bryan's room. She had felt this from the start, but hadn't liked to say anything. Now, however, something had occurred to confirm her instinct. As her patient was subject to bad dreams, she had thought it inadvisable for her to be left alone at night. So in his absence she had taken the liberty of occupying the second bed. Never in all her life had she had such a dreadful dream as came to her that night—such an extraordinarily vivid dream. Try as she would, she couldn't get it out of her mind.

This was what she had dreamed. The door of the room—Mrs. Bryan's room—had burst open and a man and a woman had dragged in an extremely tall, very young woman in a blue smock. The young woman was struggling desperately to free herself—straining with all her might to get back to the door. But the man flung her brutally on the floor, and held her down while the woman took the key out of the lock on the inside of the door, and before the girl, who seemed half stunned, could get onto her feet, they hurried out of the room, slamming the door behind them. Struggling to her feet, the wretched girl staggered to the locked door. It was plain she was in need of immediate help. She was in an agony of pain and of terror. Her poor, ringless hands tugged despairingly at the nailed window. She screamed and screamed for help until she fell down and lay writhing on the floor. Then I woke. . . . It was a *horrible* dream, Mr. Bryan. Still, I don't think I should have thought of troubling you with it had it not been for one circumstance."

"What circumstance, Nurse?"

"Well, as you and the doctor had told me my patient had been so much troubled by some dream, I tried to coax her to tell me what sort of a dream it was. She wouldn't tell me any details—she didn't seem able to bear to speak of it—but I did gather one thing, and I don't like it, Mr. Bryan."

"What was it, Nurse? Tell me."

"Well, she, too, had dreamed and dreamed more than once—of that same very tall young woman in the blue smock. She wouldn't say what was the matter with the girl, but just that she was in terrible trouble."

This was enough for John. Laura must be taken away from here. Yes, at once! The baby would have to be born elsewhere. He rushed round to the doctor. A nursing home was telephoned to; a room engaged for that very evening.

Laura's obvious relief when she was told tore John's heart. It was decided that he should drive her and the nurse to the Nursing Home immediately after tea.

To hasten the intervening two hours, John took himself off for a walk. His own sense of relief came to him as a revelation. Obviously the whole thing—Laura's recurrent dream, Prudence's name on the window pane, Tibby Mudd's maunderings—had long been far more on his nerves than he had admitted to himself. Yes, he was beginning to hate the very beauty of the place. He longed to see Laura safe in the impersonal, commonplace atmosphere of a Nursing Home. All old houses, he decided, were depressing, however beautiful. They were too heavily imbued with the past, so much of it necessarily sad. He would build a new house for Laura, one to which they could give their own happy atmosphere. Now that the weight of unacknowledged dread was lifted from his heart, John's spirits soared. He enjoyed his long tramping walk through the wet fields, and when he strode back into the garden he even burst into song as he passed under Laura's wide-open window.

"Who is Lau-ri-a? What is she?
That all our swains com——"

The song broke off in his throat at the sight of a car at the door. The doctor's car! Why was he here?

Four strides took John to the top of the stairs and into all the commotion and excitement—the relished excitement—of a precipitated crisis. Rolled-up sleeves. Boiling kettles. Elated housemaids scurrying hither and thither.

The doctor met him on the landing. "Nature has forestalled us," he said. "You'll soon be a father now."

"Can't she be taken to the Nursing Home in an ambulance at once?" asked John.

"Impossible," said the doctor. Things were going very quickly. Evidently the baby was in a hurry to come into the world. It might be here in an hour or two now. He was sorry. But, there it was—and why worry? Everything was going perfectly normally. Mrs. Bryan was the ideal patient. No one could hope for a better nurse, and he wouldn't leave the house again until all was well over. Mr. Bryan could go up now and have a look at his wife.

John saw a new Laura. Flushed, bright-eyed, exultant, she gave him a radiant smile. Then her hands clenched, her face twisted. The nurse, who didn't "hold with husbands about," bustled John out of the room. He needn't worry about atmosphere now, she whispered to him outside the door. The patient wasn't giving it a thought. The past no longer existed for her. No, except when the pains caught her back into the present, she thought only of the future—of her baby.

Downstairs, too, the doctor assured him he need have no fear of any mental agitation for his wife. Very soon, now, he would be able to give her plenty of chloroform and he would keep her right off until everything was well over. As he spoke, the nurse called the doctor to come upstairs.

John burst out of the house, and paced up and down the

lawn. The old gardener, unaware of what was going on indoors, came doddering up to him. "If you please, Sir, could I have a word with you?"

Only half attending, John heard the old man's mumblings as in a dream. He and the boy was digging out that sunken garden as the mistress had set her heart on when their spades had come on something hard. And, would you believe it? They found two " 'uman skelentons"—one ever so long. T'other that tiny—couldn't have been more than a biby. Would Mr. Bryan come and look, and please what was they to do?

John said of course the police would have to be told. He'd see to it later. He couldn't attend to anything now.

Determined to have another glimpse of Laura, he went upstairs and looked into the room. Pale as her pillow, Laura lay as though asleep. She was quite unconscious. The doctor gave John a reassuring nod. The nurse pushed him out of the room.

A boy was born at about seven o'clock. Everything was perfectly normal. It was not until the mother returned to consciousness that it began to happen. Coming to, very suddenly, Laura started up in bed in frantic perturbation. Thrusting away the nurse who had run to attend her, she pointed, at the floor. "Help *her!*" she screamed. "I'm all right. Help her. Quick! Quick! Quick!"

The doctor and the nurse did all they could to quieten the mother. They tried to force her back onto her pillows, but nothing they could say or do had the slightest effect. She fought against them with all her failing force. It took all their strength just to hold her back. They couldn't stop her from struggling, struggling to get out of bed—desperately over-straining herself. Just before her exhausted heart finally gave way, she shrieked out in a voice which wasn't her own voice—an anguished, despairing voice, "Help me! Help me! For God's sake help me! Fetch Grizel! Fetch Grizel!"

The reader may ask how the old man could have come to know some of the details I have given—for instance, certain snatches of talk between husband and wife.

I, too, asked myself that question, for—was this very imperceptive of me?—it was not until very near the end of the story that I realized that the old man to whom I listened had long, long ago been the young owner of Greystock Manor.

Bookworm

JOHN EDGELL

"On page ninety-five he suddenly saw a colored drawing which was so alive and horrible. . . ."

Mr. Purcell loved books. He adored them, and the older they were, the more he liked them. He reveled in the smooth feel of old morocco binding, the smell of crisp, yellowy pages, the romantic old-fashioned print. His widowed sister Agatha, with whom he lived, nagged him for throwing away good money on books, but Mr. Purcell shrugged this off. Why should he forgo his one pleasure?

He spent most of his spare time prowling around antiquarian bookshops hunting for bargains, for prizes to add to the collection which now burdened the shelves of his tiny room.

His fiercest ambition was to obtain a copy of a book entitled *The Burning of Beel,* which had been published in 1702 by Thomas Purcell at Bow-Yard in London. Mr. Purcell had seen this book in a footnote once, and wondered whether Thomas Purcell might be one of his ancestors. He did not know what was inside *The Burning of Beel,* but a strange voice whispered that he had to buy it.

His inquiries among booksellers and agents revealed that only one copy was known to be in existence. It belonged to an antique dealer who owned a small shop in a courtyard near the Charing Cross Road. Every Tuesday, in the late afternoon, Mr. Purcell would walk down the courtyard, staring into the dusty bow window, trying to gather courage to go in. But Mr. Purcell, who was a thin, stooped man, lacked courage. Strangely, he could never quite bring himself to enter the dark little shop.

Every time he peered through the murky window, his heart started to throb. Perhaps the book was inside, bundled away in a basement. Perhaps it was locked in a safe in the back room. Mr. Purcell knew that until he dared to ask the dealer outright he would remain in this agitated condition. Mr. Purcell owned a chain of wine stores and earned a very comfortable living. He had hardly any interest in wine, being rather more concerned with the accounts and with whether a profit was being made each financial year. He could afford to pay any reasonable price for *The Burning of Beel,* but just the same, something always prevented him from passing through the dusty glass door and meeting the dealer face to face.

Mr. Purcell visited the lonely courtyard many times. It was a shadowy Victorian yard, dirty and grubby, reminiscent of Dickensian London. Hardly a soul ever entered it, and in all the time Mr. Purcell had been visiting it, he had never seen anyone step through the door. This, he thought, was peculiar. How could the dealer make a living if he had no customers?

Mr. Purcell began to imagine that the dealer was a poor man, and would be only too happy to part with the book. This thought renewed his courage and he turned it over in his mind for several weeks. He felt that the time to meet the dealer was drawing near.

And so, one foggy January afternoon, when the lamps were lit earlier than usual and the lights burned with a misty ochre, Mr. Purcell went to the courtyard and boldly entered the shop. An iron bell tinkled, and the door closed itself behind him. Looking quickly around he saw that most of the stuff in the shop was worthless junk. Anxiously, he tapped his umbrella on the floor.

After a moment a brown curtain at the back parted and revealed a little bald man with glasses on the tip of his nose. He was very, very old, and wore woolen gloves with the fingertips cut away. He breathed asthmatically, his breath hanging in puffs on the cold air.

For a second Mr. Purcell's courage failed. He wanted to turn and leave. He desperately wanted to ask about the book, but the words stuck in his throat. The dealer coughed and clutched his chest.

"A cold day. A very cold day," he said.

Mr. Purcell nodded. "Indeed."

"Can I do anything for you?"

A moment passed. Mr. Purcell felt a sense of panic. Here was his opportunity to ask. Go on, he told himself. Ask now. Ask.

"I'm enquiring about a book," he said nervously.

The dealer seemed to hesitate. "A book? I don't have many books here. As you can see, no doubt."

Mr. Purcell looked around. There wasn't a single book in sight.

"A very special book," he said. He looked at the dealer: was it the light, or had the little man turned pale?

"A special book?" the dealer asked.

Mr. Purcell looked around at the junk in the little shop. It really was unbelievably bad. He was silent a moment. And then, he whispered the book's title: *The Burning of Beel.*

The old man took off his spectacles and rubbed them on his sleeve. "I know of no such book."

"My information is that you possess the book. Why do you deny it?"

The old man repeated, "I know of no such book."

Mr. Purcell wondered how long the pretence could go on. "My dear fellow, there's no sense in denying it. I know that you have the book. I want to know what price you are asking."

The dealer's face was quite white. He sat down and pressed a handkerchief across his brow, his fat white hands trembling; was it with anger or fear? He looked at Mr. Purcell and shook his head. "You do not know what you are asking."

"It's very simple," Mr. Purcell said, in a steady voice. "What is the price of the book?"

"Please," said the dealer, "go now. I am prepared to forget you have ever mentioned it." He took off his spectacles again and chewed the metal legs between his teeth. He looked around the shop, his bird-like eyes glittering as if he were searching for a way out.

"All right. Why do you want the book?"

"For my collection."

"You collect books on the supernatural?"

"No. I simply collect rare books."

"You are not interested in the supernatural? Then this book

isn't for you. Why buy a book that does not interest you?"

Mr. Purcell grit his teeth. "Because I want the book. I think the publisher may have been an ancestor of mine—Thomas Purcell."

"Thomas Purcell!" The dealer seemed very startled. He stood up, rubbing the palms of his hands on his trousers.

He stared coldly at Mr. Purcell for a while. A silence fell.

"I cannot sell the book, because there is another buyer."

"Another buyer?" Mr. Purcell smiled. "I'll offer more. How much is he offering for it?"

"Oh, he is not offering anything, he simply wants the book."

"But that's absurd. I'm offering money. Sell the book to me. I'll give you a hundred pounds!" Mr. Purcell began to feel reckless, his head was spinning as if he were drunk.

The dealer walked up and down the shop. His head, which he was shaking from side to side, reminded Mr. Purcell of the head of a sparrow picking at crusts.

"No. I cannot sell. I'm sorry. Please go."

Mr. Purcell said with deadly calm, "A hundred pounds, man. That's a lot of money."

For the first time the dealer smiled. "The other interested party isn't offering money. He isn't offering anything. I'd gladly sell you the book . . . if I could."

"Then why don't you? For God's sake, man, I must have that book."

The dealer sat down again, silhouetted in a chair near the window.

"Why do you think I keep a shop in this forsaken courtyard? Why do you imagine I live like this? Because I enjoy being a poor man? No, no, it is nothing like that. You must understand that I am here because I have to be. Because here it is less easy for anyone to find me. Because . . . because this other interested party will have some trouble in seeking me out."

Mr. Purcell hardly knew what to say in his exasperation. "Are you afraid of this other person? If you are, why don't you sell the book to me? Then you'd have nothing more to fear."

The dealer laughed bitterly. "It would solve nothing if I sold you the book. I cannot sell it because it is not mine to sell!"

Mr. Purcell had no idea what he was talking about. Someone else wanted the book, but was not offering money. So why didn't the old fool sell the book to Purcell? Clearly he was afraid of this other person—but why? And if the book did not belong to him, then who owned it?

"Sell it to me," Mr. Purcell shouted, leaning forward, catching him by the wrist. "Dammit, man, I want that book!"

The old man struggled feebly. Mr. Purcell glanced through the dirty window. Outside, the fog was thicker than ever. It was thick enough to hide anything. Anything at all.

It was over in a flash. Mr. Purcell did not even remember doing it. The body of the old man lay on the floor, the neck broken from the sudden blow. In his hands, Mr. Purcell held a heavy bronze statuette of a soldier. As he looked down the skin of the old man's face seemed to wither and grow strange: he might have been two hundred years old.

Quickly he drew down the blind and put the "Closed" sign up on the window. He hurried through the brown curtain into the back of the shop. As he had imagined a safe stood in the corner and, as luck would have it, a key lay on top. He opened the steel door and rummaged through several sheets of paper before he found the book. It was wrapped in a cellophane envelope.

Trembling, he removed it and thrust it inside his coat. On his way out he hardly stopped to look at the old man's body which now lay in a pool of darkening blood seeping from the mouth.

The little iron bell rang again as Mr. Purcell left. He soon lost himself in the fog, and covered a good distance from the shop. He found his way to the Strand underground station and mixed with the noisy evening rush-hour crowds. On his way home he realized, with surprise, that he felt nothing at having killed the dealer. He had never killed in his life before and was astonished that it had been so easy. So very easy.

In the privacy of his study Mr. Purcell took the book, *The Burning of Beel,* from the envelope and opened it carefully. The wonderful smell of the old paper, damp with age, rose to his nostrils. This was the gem of his entire collection; a beautiful and rare book, his alone to cherish. And on the title page was scrawled in faded brown ink: "First published by me, Thos. Purcell, 1702."

He turned the pages, and read here and there. Much of it was about those creatures that are neither living nor dead, the undead, half-shapes that come to stalk our nightmares. Mr. Purcell did not believe a word of such superstitious nonsense, and wondered whether Thomas Purcell himself had believed it.

On page ninety-five he suddenly saw a colored drawing which was so alive and horrible that he was riveted by it. From the yellow page, a man—or something like a man—stared at him, a hunched figure with red eyes, long dark hair, and a crippled leg. Mr. Purcell felt himself drawn against his will into those eyes and the reptilian loathing and malice that was contained in them. Sweating, he read the caption under the picture which said: "Balthazar Beel, born in 1615, possessed of unnatural and unholy powers, a wicked and vile creature. In 1667 an attempt was made to burn him at the stake."

Mr. Purcell closed the book and shut his eyes. What did it mean, an attempt had been made to burn him? Had he been burned or not? Had the flames gone out? Mr. Purcell replaced the book inside the envelope, locked it in the drawer of his desk and then went downstairs to take supper with his sister Agatha.

For the next few weeks Mr. Purcell examined every page of *The Burning of Beel.* It was a perfect specimen of its kind, in beautiful condition, its binding still immaculate. He was overjoyed with it and it hardly mattered that the newspapers still clamored about the brutal murder of the old man, whose name no one knew. Mr. Purcell felt safe: there was nothing to link him with the affair, and although a woman claimed to have seen someone loitering near the courtyard a few times, this caused him no special anxiety. He ate and slept well and the event began to fade from his mind. He even began to think he had not committed the crime, and when his sister remarked that hanging was too good for the murderer, he found himself agreeing with her wholeheartedly.

Mr. Purcell often went to the British Museum to explore the catalogues there. Only in the British Museum did he feel completely at home, in an atmosphere thick with reading and books. It was in the Museum, in the Reading Room, that he had his first unpleasant experience.

While examining a catalogue, he suddenly imagined someone staring at him. He looked around, but although he could see nothing, the odd feeling persisted. He went outside and walked through Bloomsbury, but still he had this strange sensation. He entered a public house, ordered a glass of brandy, and sat down in a corner of the saloon bar. In the mirror facing him he suddenly saw, or thought he saw, the flash of a familiar face—but he could not be sure. When he looked again there was nothing.

At first he imagined that the police might be on his trail. But this was a ridiculous thought. There was absolutely nothing to link him with the crime. He had not left his umbrella behind;

he had worn gloves, so there were no fingerprints; and he had locked the safe behind him. Unless the police knew about the book, they could not know that there had been a robbery.

After half an hour he hailed a taxi and went home. In the taxi he glanced several times through the rear window.

What he was looking for he did not know.

When he arrived home, his sister was in the drawing room, reading a magazine.

"Been to the Museum, Rupert?" she asked.

"Indeed," he answered.

"By the way, someone called for you while you were out."

"Oh yes? Anyone interesting?"

"He didn't leave a name. I've never seen him before. Strange-looking man."

"Strange?" Mr. Purcell poured himself a glass of brandy.

"He said he'd come back. I don't know what he wanted."

Mr. Purcell sat down and sighed. He hated visitors—unless it happened to be someone with an interesting book to sell. When he had finished his drink, he went up to his study. The room was cold. He lit the fire, rubbed his hands, and took down *The Burning of Beel.* It was an amusing tale of witches and ghouls, ghosts and magicians—a lot of nonsense. And there was the drawing of Balthazar Beel himself, which reminded Mr. Purcell that he had intended to check the name at the Museum to see if anything else was known.

Mr. Purcell turned the pages. Suddenly, he again had the strange sensation that he was being watched: something physical, malignant, seemed to threaten him from nearby. He stood up, looked quickly around the room, but found nothing out of place. He stared out of the window. Under the lamppost opposite, a man was standing, the collar of his coat turned up. He seemed to be staring up at Mr. Purcell, but perhaps this was an optical illusion. Mr. Purcell could not see the man's eyes properly, and he could not tell for sure.

Just the same, he drew the curtain and returned to his book. But he could not concentrate now. He felt as if the air had been poisoned. He left the study and went down to talk to Agatha. But she had gone out.

It was late afternoon and the street lamps were already lit. Mr. Purcell drank another glass of brandy and wondered who could have called on him that afternoon. With a tingle of shock, he remembered that the dealer had said someone else was interested in obtaining the book. Could this other person now know that he had the book? But, no, how could that be? Could it have been this other person who had called on him? Mr. Purcell felt strangely vulnerable.

He must take things easy and relax. Possibly he was experiencing some reaction from the murder, an attack of nerves, perhaps: a result of strain.

He drank another brandy. It warmed his chest but did not relax him. He was about to pour another glass when the doorbell rang. Suddenly he froze. Not a single muscle in his body moved. He held his breath. It shrilled again and again, and then at last he heard footsteps going away from the house—one foot dragging slightly, scraping against the concrete. Cautiously, Mr. Purcell peeped through the curtain. He saw the dim figure of a man go down the street. He drank some more brandy; his head felt weary.

After supper he talked to Agatha for a time and then, when she went to bed, he retired to his study. He decided to ignore *The Burning of Beel,* and took out a paperback crime thriller—the perfect remedy for bad nerves, a good, short relaxing read. It was a story of a badly bungled murder, with suspicions being thrown on all six guests at a country house. Halfway through, almost asleep, Mr. Purcell heard a noise on the stairs. It must be Agatha, he thought, going for a glass of water.

Yet the noise seemed to come from just outside the door of his study. He sat up, now wide awake. To his horror, he saw the handle of the door being turned, turned very slowly. His study seemed to grow very hot.

"Who is it?" he called, nervously.

There was a long, scraping sound, as if a fingernail had been drawn across the wood. Mr. Purcell felt as if a knife had been drawn across his flesh. He rose from his chair. The door was opening slowly, a white hand slid around its side.

"Who is it?" Mr. Purcell picked up the poker, sweating in the rising heat. He stepped back. He raised the poker in anticipation. If it was a thief, he was ready for him. But Mr. Purcell had the feeling that it was something else.

Slowly, the door opened wide, the study felt like a furnace. Mr. Purcell felt the poker slip from his fingers and drop noisily on the floor. There in the doorway, stood a man. A familiar man. Or something like a man.

Covered with charred flesh, the hunched figure stared with bloodshot eyes. Mr. Purcell gasped.

The figure spoke.

"My name is Beel. Balthazar Beel. I've come for my book."

And dragging one leg behind, it inched toward him.

Forever and the Earth

RAY BRADBURY

"Thomas Wolfe wrote of the past, the future," declared the old man. "He's the man—the necessary man, to write of time, change, huge things like nebulae and galactic war. . . . Never fear, I will find him!"

After seventy years of writing short stories that never sold, Mr. Henry William Field arose one night at eleven-thirty and burned ten million words. He carried the manuscripts downstairs through his dark old mansion and threw them into the furnace.

"That's that," he said, and thinking about his lost art and his misspent life, he put himself to bed, among his rich antiques. "My mistake was in ever trying to picture this wild world of A.D. 2257. The rockets, the atom wonders, the travels to planets and double suns. Nobody can do it. Everyone's tried. All of our modern authors have failed."

Space was too big for them, and rockets too swift, and atomic science too instantaneous, he thought. But at least the other writers, while failing, had been published, while he, in his idle wealth, had used the years of his life for nothing.

After an hour of feeling this way, he fumbled through the night rooms to his library and switched on a green hurricane lamp. At random, from a collection untouched in fifty years, he selected a book. It was a book three centuries yellow and three centuries brittle, but he settled into it and read hungrily until dawn. . . .

At nine the next morning, Henry William Field staggered from his library, called his servants, televised lawyers, scientists, literateurs.

"Come at once!" he cried.

By noon, a dozen people had stepped into the study where Henry William Field sat, very disreputable and hysterical with an odd, feeding joy, unshaven and feverish. He clutched a thick book in his brittle arms and laughed if anyone even said good morning.

"Here you see a book," he said at last, holding it out, "written by a giant, a man born in Asheville, North Carolina, in the year 1900. Long gone to dust, he published four huge novels. He was a whirlwind. He lifted up mountains and collected winds. He left a trunk of penciled manuscripts behind when he lay in bed at Johns Hopkins Hospital in Baltimore in the year 1938, on September fifteenth, and died of pneumonia, an ancient and awful disease."

They looked at the book.

Look Homeward, Angel.

He drew forth three more. *Of Time and the River. The Web and the Rock. You Can't Go Home Again.*

"By Thomas Wolfe," said the old man. "Three centuries cold in the North Carolina earth."

"You mean you've called us simply to see four books by a dead man?" his friends protested.

"More than that! I've called you because I feel Tom Wolfe's the man, the necessary man, to write of space, of time, huge things like nebulae and galactic war, meteors and planets, all the dark things he loved and put on paper were like this. He was born out of his time. He needed really *big* things to play with and never found them on Earth. He should have been born this afternoon instead of one hundred thousand mornings ago."

"I'm afraid you're a bit late," said Professor Bolton.

"I don't intend to be late!" snapped the old man. "I will *not* be frustrated by reality. You, professor, have experimented with time-travel. I expect you to finish your time machine as soon as possible. Here's a check, a blank check, fill it in. If you need more money, ask for it. You've done *some* traveling already, haven't you?"

"A few years, yes, but nothing like centuries—"

"We'll *make* it centuries! You others"—he swept them with a fierce and shining glance—"will work with Bolton. I *must* have Thomas Wolfe."

"What!" They fell back before him.

"Yes," he said. "That's the plan. Wolfe is to be brought to me. We will collaborate in the task of describing the flight from Earth to Mars, as only he could describe it!"

They left him in his library with his books, turning the dry pages, nodding to himself. "Yes. Oh, dear Lord yes, Tom's the boy, Tom is the *very* boy for this."

The months passed slowly. Days showed a maddening reluctance to leave the calendar, and weeks lingered on until Mr. Henry William Field began to scream silently.

At the end of four months, Mr. Field awoke one midnight. The phone was ringing. He put his hand out in the darkness.

"Yes?"

"This is Professor Bolton calling."

"Yes, Bolton?"

"I'll be leaving in an hour," said the voice.

"Leaving? Leaving where? Are you quitting? You can't do that!"

"Please, Mr. Field, leaving means *leaving.*"

"You mean, you're actually going?"

"Within the hour."

"To 1938? To September fifteenth?"

"Yes!"

"You're sure you've the date fixed correctly? You'll arrive before he dies? Be sure of it! Good Lord, you'd better get there a good hour before his death, don't you think?"

"*Two* hours. On the way back, we'll mark time in Bermuda, borrow ten days of free-floating continuum, inject him, tan him, swim him, vitaminize him, make him well."

"I'm so excited I can't hold the phone. Good luck, Bolton. Bring him through safely!"

"Thank you, sir. Good-bye."

The phone clicked.

Mr. Henry William Field lay through the ticking night. He thought of Tom Wolfe as a lost brother to be lifted intact from under a cold, chiseled stone, to be restored to blood and fire and speaking. He trembled each time he thought of Bolton whirling on the time wind back to other calendars and other days, bearing medicines to change flesh and save souls.

Tom, he thought, faintly, in the half-awake warmth of an old man calling after his favorite and long-gone child, Tom, where are you tonight, Tom? Come along now, we'll help you through, you've got to come, there's need for you. I couldn't do it, Tom, none of us here can. So the next best thing to doing it myself, Tom, is helping you to do it. You can play with rockets like jackstraws, Tom, and you can have the stars, like a handful of crystals. Anything your heart asks, it's here. You'd like the fire and the travel, Tom, it was made for you. Oh, we've a pale lot of writers today, I've read them all, Tom, and they're not like you. I've waded in libraries of their stuff and they've never touched space, Tom; we need *you* for that! Give an old man his wish then, for God knows I've waited all my life for myself or some other to write the really great book about the stars, and I've waited in vain. So, wherever you are tonight, Tom Wolfe, make yourself tall. It's that book you were going to write. It's that good book the critics said was in you when you stopped breathing. Here's your chance, will you do it, Tom? Will you listen and come through to us, will you do that tonight, and be here in the morning when I wake? Will you, Tom?

His eyelids closed down over the fever and the demand. His tongue stopped quivering in his sleeping mouth.

The clock struck four.

Awakening to the white coolness of morning, he felt the excitement rising and welling in himself. He did not wish to blink, for fear that the thing which awaited him somewhere in the house might run off and slam a door, gone forever. His hands reached up to clutch his thin chest.

Far away . . . footsteps . . .

A series of doors opened and shut. Two men entered the bedroom.

Field could hear them breathe. Their footsteps took on

identities. The first steps were those of a spider, small and precise: Bolton. The second steps were those of a big man, a large man, a heavy man.

"Tom?" cried the old man. He did not open his eyes.

"Yes," said a voice, at last.

Tom Wolfe burst the seams of Field's imagination, as a huge child bursts the lining of a too-small coat.

"Tom Wolfe, let me look at you!" If Field said it once, he said it a dozen times as he fumbled from bed, shaking violently. "Put up the blinds, for God's sake, I want to see this! Tom Wolfe, is that *you*?"

Tom Wolfe looked down from his tall thick body, with big hands out to balance himself in a world that was strange. He looked at the old man and the room and his mouth was trembling.

"You're just as they said you were, Tom!"

Thomas Wolfe began to laugh and the laughing was huge, for he must have thought himself insane or in a nightmare, and he came to the old man and touched him and he looked at Professor Bolton and felt of himself, his arms and legs, he coughed experimentally and touched his own brow. "My fever's gone," he said. "I'm not sick anymore."

"Of course not, Tom."

"What a night," said Tom Wolfe. "It hasn't been easy. I thought I was sicker than any man ever was. I felt myself floating and I thought, This is fever. I felt myself traveling, and thought, I'm dying fast. A man came to me. I thought, This is the Lord's messenger. He took my hands. I smelled electricity. I flew up and over, and I saw a brass city. I thought, I've arrived. This is the city of heaven, there is the Gate! I'm numb from head to toe, like someone left in the snow to freeze. I've got to laugh and do things or I might think myself insane. You're not God, are you? You don't look like Him."

The old man laughed. "No, no, Tom, not God, but playing at it. I'm Field." He laughed again. "Lord, listen to me. I said it as if you should know who Field is. Field, the financier, Tom, bow low, kiss my ring finger. I'm Henry Field. I like your work, I brought you here. Come along."

The old man drew him to an immense crystal window.

"Do you see those lights in the sky, Tom?"

"Yes, sir."

"Those fireworks?"

"Yes."

"They're not what you think, son. It's not July Fourth, Tom. Not in the usual way. Every day's Independence Day now. Man has declared his Freedom from Earth. Gravitation without representation has been overthrown. The Revolt has long since been successful. That green Roman Candle's going to Mars. That red fire, that's the Venus rocket. And the others, you see the yellow and the blue? Rockets, all of them!"

Thomas Wolfe gazed up like an immense child caught amid the colorized glories of a July evening when the set-pieces are awhirl with phosphorus and glitter and barking explosion.

"What year is this?"

"The year of the rocket. Look here." And the old man touched some flowers that bloomed at his touch. The blossoms were like blue and white fire. They burned and sparkled their cold, long petals. The blooms were two feet wide, and they were the color of an autumn moon. "Moon-flowers," said the old man. "From the other side of the moon." He brushed them and they dripped away into a silver rain, a shower of white sparks on the air. "The year of the rocket. That's a title for you, Tom. That's why we brought you here, we've need of you. You're the only man could handle the sun without being burnt to a ridiculous cinder. We want you to juggle the sun, Tom, and the stars, and whatever else you see on your trip to Mars."

"Mars?" Thomas Wolfe turned to seize the old man's arm, bending down to him, searching his face in unbelief.

"Tonight. You leave at six o'clock."

The old man held a fluttering pink ticket on the air, waiting for Tom to think to take it.

It was five in the afternoon. "Of course, of course I appreciate what you've done," cried Thomas Wolfe.

"Sit down, Tom. Stop walking around."

"Let me finish, Mr. Field, let me get through with this, I've got to say it."

"We've been arguing for hours," pleaded Mr. Field, exhaustedly.

They had talked from breakfast until lunch until tea, they had wandered through a dozen rooms and ten dozen arguments, they had perspired and grown cold and perspired again.

"It all comes down to this," said Thomas Wolfe, at last. "I can't stay here, Mr. Field. I've got to go back. This isn't my time. You've no right to interfere—"

"But I—"

"I was deep in my work, my best yet to come, and now you run me off three centuries. Mr. Field, I want you to call Mr. Bolton back. I want you to have him put me in his machine, whatever it is, and return me to 1938, my rightful place and year. That's all I ask of you."

"But don't you *want* to see Mars?"

"With all my heart. But I know it isn't for me. It would throw my writing off. I'd have a huge handful of experience that I couldn't fit into my other writing when I went home."

"You don't understand, Tom, you don't understand at all."

"I understand that you're selfish."

"Selfish? Yes," said the old man. "For myself, and for others, very selfish."

"I want to go home."

"Listen to me, Tom."

"Call Mr. Bolton."

"Tom, I don't want to have to tell you this. I thought I wouldn't have to, that it wouldn't be necessary. Now, you leave me only this alternative." The old man's right hand fetched hold of a curtained wall, swept back the drapes, revealing a large white screen, and dialed a number, a series of numbers. The screen flickered into vivid color, the lights of the room darkened, darkened, and a graveyard took line before their eyes.

"What are you doing?" demanded Wolfe, striding forward, staring at the screen.

"I don't like this at all," said the old man. "Look there."

The graveyard lay in midafternoon light, the light of summer. From the screen drifted the smell of summer earth, granite, and the odor of a nearby creek. From the trees, a bird called. Red and yellow flowers nodded among the stones, and the screen moved, the sky rotated, the old man twisted a dial for emphasis, and in the center of the screen, growing large, coming closer, yet larger, and now filling their senses, was a dark granite mass; and Thomas Wolfe, looking up in the dim room, ran his eyes over the chiseled words, once, twice, three times, gasped, and read again, for there was his name:

THOMAS WOLFE.

And the date of his birth and the date of his death, and the flowers and green ferns smelling sweetly on the air of the cold room.

"Turn it off," he said.

"I'm sorry, Tom."

"Turn it off, turn it off! I don't believe it."

"It's there."

The screen went black and now the entire room as a

Six o'clock. The sun setting. The sky turning to wine. The big house quiet. The old man shivering in the heat until Professor Bolton entered. "Bolton, how is he getting on, how was he at the port; tell me?"

Bolton smiled. "What a monster he is, so big they had to make a special uniform for him! You should've seen him, walking around, lifting up everything, sniffing like a great hound, talking, his eyes looking at everyone, excited as a ten-year-old!"

"God bless him, oh, God bless him! Bolton, can you keep him here as long as you say?"

Bolton frowned, "He doesn't belong here, you know. If our power should falter, he'd be snapped back to his own time, like a puppet on a rubber band. We'll try and keep him, I assure you."

"You've got to, you understand, you can't let him go back until he's finished with his book. You've—"

"Look," said Bolton. He pointed to the sky. On it was a silver rocket.

"Is that him?" asked the old man.

"That's Tom Wolfe," replied Bolton. "Going to Mars."

"Give 'em hell, Tom, give 'em hell!" shouted the old man, lifting both fists.

They watched the rocket fire into space.

By midnight, the story was coming through.

Henry William Field sat in his library. On his desk was a machine that hummed. It repeated words that were being written out beyond the moon. It scrawled them in black pencil, in facsimile of Tom Wolfe's fevered hand a million miles away. The old man waited for a pile of them to collect and then he seized them and read them aloud to the room where Bolton and the servants stood listening. He read the words about space and time and travel, about a large man and a large journey and how it was in the long midnight and coldness of space, and how a man could be hungry enough to take all of it and ask for more. He read the words that were full of fire and thunder and mystery.

Space was like October, wrote Thomas Wolfe. He said things about its darkness and its loneliness and man so small in it. The eternal and timeless October, was one of the things he said. And then he told of the rocket itself, the smell and the feel of the metal of the rocket, and the sense of destiny and wild exultancy to at last leave Earth behind, all problems and all sadnesses, and go seeking a bigger problem and a bigger sadness. Oh, it was fine writing, and it said what had to be said about space and man and his small rockets out there alone.

The old man read until he was hoarse, and then Bolton read, and then the others, far into the night, when the machine stopped transcribing words and they knew that Tom Wolfe was in bed, then, on the rocket, flying to Mars, probably not asleep, no, he wouldn't sleep for hours yet, no, lying awake, like a boy the night before a circus, not believing the big jeweled black tent is up and the circus is on, with ten billion performers on the high wires and the invisible trapezes of space.

"There," breathed the old man, gentling aside the last pages of the first chapter. "What do you think of that, Bolton?"

"It's good."

"Good, hell!" shouted Field. "It's wonderful! Read it again, sit down, read it again, damn you!"

It kept coming through, one day following another, for ten hours at a time. The stack of yellow papers on the floor, scribbled on, grew immense in a week, unbelievable in two weeks, absolutely impossible in a month.

"Listen to this!" cried the old man, and read.

"And this!" he said.

"And this chapter here, and this little novel here, it just came through, Bolton, titled 'The Space War,' a complete novel on how it feels to fight a space war. Tom's been talking to people, soldiers, officers, men, veterans of space. He's got it all here. And here's a chapter called 'The Long Midnight,' and here's one on the Negro colonization of Mars, and here's a character sketch of a Martian, absolutely priceless!"

Bolton cleared his throat. "Mr. Field?"

"Yes, yes, don't bother me."

"I've some bad news, sir."

Field jerked his gray head up. "What? The time element?"

"You'd better tell Wolfe to hurry his work. The connection may break sometime this week," said Bolton, softly.

"I'll give you anything, anything if you keep it going!"

"It's not money, Mr. Field. It's just plain physics right now. I'll do everything I can. But you'd better warn him."

The old man shriveled in his chair and was small. "But you can't take him away from me now, not when he's doing so well! You should see the outline he sent through an hour ago, the stories, the sketches. Here, here's one on spatial tides, another on meteors. Here's a short novel begun, called 'Thistledown and Fire'—"

"I'm sorry."

"If we lose him now, can we get him again?"

"I'd be afraid to tamper too much."

The old man was frozen. "Only one thing to do then. Arrange to have Wolfe type his work, if possible, or dictate it, to save time; rather than have him use pencil and paper, he's got to use a machine of some sort. See to it!"

The machine ticked away by the hour into the night and into the dawn and through the day. The old man slept only in faint dozes, blinking awake when the machine stuttered to life, and all of space and travel and existence came to him through the mind of another:

". . . *the great starred meadows of space* . . ."

The machine jumped.

"Keep at it Tom, show them!" The old man waited.

The phone rang.

It was Bolton.

"We can't keep it up, Mr. Field. The continuum device will absolute out within one hour."

"Do something!"

"I can't."

The teletype chattered. In a cold fascination, in a horror, the old man watched the black lines form.

". . . *the Martian cities, immense and unbelievable, as numerous as stones thrown from some great mountain in a rushing and incredible avalanche, resting at last in shining mounds* . . ."

"Tom!" cried the old man.

"Now," said Bolton, on the phone.

The teletype hesitated, typed a word, and fell silent.

"Tom!" screamed the old man.

He shook the teletype.

"It's no use," said the telephone voice. "He's gone. I'm shutting off the time machine."

"No! Leave it on!"

"But—"

"You heard me—leave it! We're not sure he's gone."

"He is. It's no use, we're wasting energy."

"Waste it, then!"

He slammed the phone down.

He turned to the teletype, to the unfinished sentence.

"Come on, Tom, they can't get rid of you that way, you

won't let them, will you, boy, come on. Tom, show them, you're big, you're bigger than time or space or their damned machines, you're strong and you've a will like iron, Tom, show them, don't let them send you back!"

The teletype snapped one key.

The old man bleated. "Tom! You *are* there, aren't you? Can you still write? Write, Tom, keep it coming, as long as you keep it rolling, Tom, they *can't* send you back!"

The, typed the machine.

"More, Tom, more!"

Odors of, clacked the machine.

"Yes?"

Mars, typed the machine, and paused. A minute's silence. The machine spaced, skipped a paragraph, and began:

The odors of Mars, the cinnamons and cold spice winds, the winds of cloudy dust and winds of powerful bone and ancient pollen—

"Tom, you're still alive!"

For answer the machine, in the next ten hours, slammed out six chapters of "Flight Before Fury" in a series of fevered explosions.

"Today makes six weeks, Bolton, six whole weeks, Tom gone, on Mars, through the Asteroids. Look here, the manuscripts. Ten thousand words a day, he's driving himself, I don't know when he sleeps, or if he eats, I don't care, he doesn't either, he only wants to get it done, because he knows the time is short."

"I can't understand it," said Bolton. "The power failed because our relays wore out. It took us three days to manufacture and replace the particular channel relays necessary to keep the Time Element steady, and yet Wolfe hung on.

There's a personal factor here, Lord knows what, we didn't take into account. Wolfe lives here, in this time, when he *is* here, and can't be snapped back, after all. Time isn't as flexible as we imagined. We used the wrong simile. It's not like a rubber band. More like osmosis; the penetration of membranes by liquids, from Past to Present, but we've got to send him back, can't keep him here, there'd be a void there, a derangement. The one thing that really keeps him here now is himself, his drive, his desire, his work. After it's over he'll go back as naturally as pouring water from a glass."

"I don't care about reasons, all I know is Tom is finishing it. He has the old fire and description, and something else, something more, a searching of values that supersede time and space. He's done a study of a woman left behind on Earth while the damn rocket heroes leap into space that's beautiful, objective, and subtle; he calls it 'Day of the Rocket,' and it is nothing more than an afternoon of a typical suburban housewife who lives as her ancestral mothers lived, in a house, raising her children, her life not much different from a cavewoman's, in the midst of the splendor of science and the trumpetings of space projectiles; a true and steady and subtle study of her wishes and frustrations. Here's another manuscript, called 'The Indians,' in which he refers to the Martians as Cherokees and Iroquois and Blackfoots, the Indian nations of space, destroyed and driven back. Have a drink, Bolton, have a drink!"

Tom Wolfe returned to Earth at the end of eight weeks.

He arrived in fire as he had left in fire, and his huge steps were burned across space, and in the library of Henry William Field's house were towers of yellow paper, with lines of black scribble and type on them, and these were to be separated out into the six sections of a masterwork that, through endurance, and a knowing that the sands were dwindling from the glass, had mushroomed day after day.

Tom Wolfe came back to Earth and stood in the library of Henry William Field's house and looked at the massive outpourings of his heart and his hand and when the old man said, "Do you want to read it, Tom?" he shook his great head and replied, putting back his thick mane of dark hair with his big pale hand, "No. I don't dare start on it. If I did, I'd want to take it home with me. And I can't do that, can I?"

"No, Tom, you can't."

"No matter *how* much I wanted to?"

"No, that's the way it is. You never wrote another novel in that year, Tom. What was written here must stay here, what was written there must stay there. There's no touching it."

"I see." Tom sank down into a chair with a great sigh. "I'm tired. I'm mightily tired. It's been hard, but it's been good. What day is it?"

"This is the fifty-sixth day."

"The *last* day?"

The old man nodded and they were both silent awhile.

"Back to 1938 in the stone cemetery," said Tom Wolfe, eyes shut. "I don't like that. I wish I didn't know about that, it's a horrible thing to know." His voice faded and he put his big hands over his face and held them tightly there.

The door opened. Bolton let himself in and stood behind Tom Wolfe's chair, a small phial in his hand.

"What's that?" asked the old man.

"An extinct virus. Pneumonia. Very ancient and very evil," said Bolton. "When Mr. Wolfe came through, I had to cure him of his illness, of course, which was immensely easy with the techniques we know today, in order to put him in working condition for his job, Mr. Field. I kept this pneumonia culture.

Now that he's going back, he'll have to be reinoculated with the disease."

"Otherwise?"

Tom Wolfe looked up.

"Otherwise, he'd get well, in 1938."

Tom Wolfe arose from his chair. "You mean, get well, walk around, back there, be well, and cheat the mortician?"

"That's what I mean."

Tom Wolfe stared at the phial and one of his hands twitched. "What if I destroyed the virus and refused to let you inoculate me?"

"You can't do that!"

"But—supposing?"

"You'd ruin things."

"What things?"

"The pattern, life, the way things are and were, the things that can't be changed. You can't disrupt it. There's only one sure thing, you're to die, and I'm to see to it."

Wolfe looked at the door. "I could run off."

"We control the machine. You wouldn't get out of the house. I'd have you back here, by force, and inoculated. I anticipated some such trouble when the time came; there are five men waiting down below. One shout from me—you see, it's useless. There, that's better. Here now."

Wolfe had moved back and now had turned to look at the old man and the window and this huge house. "I'm afraid I must apologize. I don't want to die. So very much I don't want to die."

The old man came to him and took his hand. "Think of it this way: you've had two more months than anyone could expect from life, and you've turned out another book, a last book, a fine book, think of that."

"I want to thank you for this," said Thomas Wolfe, gravely.

"I want to thank both of you. I'm ready." He rolled up his sleeve. "The inoculation."

And while Bolton bent to his task, with his free hand Thomas Wolfe penciled two black lines across the top of the first manuscript and went on talking:

"There's a passage from one of my old books," he said, scowling to remember it. ". . . *of wandering forever and the Earth . . . Who owns the Earth? Did we want the Earth? That we should wander on it? Did we need the Earth that we were never still upon it? Whoever needs the Earth shall have the Earth; he shall be upon it, he shall rest within a little place, he shall dwell in one small room forever. . . .*"

Wolfe was finished with the remembering.

"Here's my last book," he said, and on the empty yellow paper facing the manuscript he blocked out vigorous huge black letter with pressures of the pencil:

FOREVER AND THE EARTH, by Thomas Wolfe.

He picked up a ream of it and held it tightly in his hands, against his chest, for a moment. "I wish I could take it back with me. It's like parting with my son." He gave it a slap and put it aside and immediately thereafter gave his quick hand into that of his employer, and strode across the room, Bolton after him, until he reached the door where he stood framed in the late-afternoon light, huge and magnificent. "Good-bye, good-bye!" he cried.

The door slammed. Tom Wolfe was gone.

They found him wandering in the hospital corridor.

"Mr. Wolfe!"

"What?"

"Mr. Wolfe, you gave us a scare, we thought you were gone!"

"Gone?"

"Where did you go?"

"Where? Where?" He let himself be led through the midnight corridors. "Where? Oh, if I *told* you where, you'd never believe."

"Here's your bed, you shouldn't have left it."

Deep into the white death bed, which had the hospital odor in it; the bed which, as he touched it, folded him into fumes and white starched coldness.

"Mars, Mars," whispered the huge man, late at night. "My best, my very best, my really fine book, yet to be written, yet to be printed, in another year, three centuries away . . ."

"You're tired."

"Do you really think so?" murmured Thomas Wolfe. "Was it a dream? Perhaps. A good dream."

His breathing faltered. Thomas Wolfe was dead.

In the passing years, flowers are found on Tom Wolfe's grave. And this is not unusual, for many people travel to linger there. But these flowers appear each night. They seem to drop from the sky. They are the color of an autumn moon, their blossoms are immense, and they burn and sparkle their cold, long petals in a blue and white fire. And when the dawn wind blows they drip away into a silver rain, a shower of white sparks on the air. Tom Wolfe has been dead many, many years, but these flowers never cease. . . .

Cool Air

H. P. LOVECRAFT

It is a mistake to fancy that horror is associated inextricably with darkness, silence, and solitude.

You ask me to explain why I am afraid of a draught of cool air; why I shiver more than others upon entering a cold room, and seem nauseated and repelled when the chill of evening creeps through the heat of a mild autumn day. There are those who say I respond to cold as others do to a bad odor, and I am the last to deny the impression. What I will do is to relate the most horrible circumstances I ever encountered, and leave it to you to judge whether or not this forms a suitable explanation of my peculiarity.

It is a mistake to fancy that horror is associated inextricably with darkness, silence, and solitude. I found it in the glare of midafternoon, in the clangor of a metropolis, and in the teeming midst of a shabby and commonplace roominghouse with a prosaic landlady and two stalwart men by my side. In the spring of 1923 I had secured some dreary and unprofitable magazine work in the city of New York, and being unable to pay any substantial rent, began drifting from one cheap boarding establishment to another in search of a room which might combine the qualities of decent cleanliness, endurable furnishings, and very reasonable price. It soon developed that I had only a choice between different evils, but after a time I came upon a house in West Fourteenth Street which disgusted me much less than the others I had sampled.

The place was a four-story mansion of brownstone, dating apparently from the late forties, and fitted with woodwork and marble whose stained and sullied splendor argued a descent from high levels of tasteful opulence. In the rooms, large and lofty, and decorated with impossible paper and ridiculously ornate stucco cornices, there lingered a depressing mustiness and hint of obscure cookery; but the floors were clean, the linen tolerably regular, and the hot water not too often cold or turned off, so that I came to regard it as at least a bearable place to hibernate 'til one might really live again. The landlady, a slatternly, almost bearded Spanish woman named Herrero, did not annoy me with gossip or with criticisms of the late-burning electric light in my third-floor front-hall room; and my fellow-lodgers were as quiet and uncommunicative as one might desire, being mostly Spaniards a little above the coarsest and crudest grade. Only the din of streetcars in the thoroughfare below proved a serious annoyance.

I had been there about three weeks when the first odd incident occurred. One evening at about eight I heard a spattering on the floor and became suddenly aware that I had been smelling the pungent odor of ammonia for some time.

Looking about, I saw that the ceiling was wet and dripping, the soaking apparently proceeding from a corner on the side toward the street. Anxious to stop the matter at its source, I hastened to the basement to tell the landlady, and was assured by her that the trouble would quickly be set right.

"Doctair Muñoz," she cried as she rushed upstairs ahead of me, "he have speel hees chemicals. He ees too seeck for doctair heemself—seecker and seecker all the time—but he weel not have no othair for help. Hees vairy queer in hees seeckness—all day he take funnee-smelling baths, and he cannot get excite or warm. All hees own housework he do—hees leetle room are full of bottles and machines, and he do not work as doctair. But he was great once—my fathair in Barcelona have hear of heem—and only joost now he feex a arm of the plumber that get hurt of sudden. He nevair go out, only on roof, and my boy Estaban he breeng heem hees food and laundry and mediceens and chemicals. My God, the salammoniac that man use for to keep heem cool!"

Mrs. Herrero disappeared up the staircase to the fourth floor, and I returned to my room. The ammonia ceased to drip, and as I cleaned up what had spilled and opened the window for air, I heard the landlady's heavy footsteps above me. Dr. Muñoz I had never heard, save for certain sounds as of some gasoline-driven mechanism, since his step was soft and gentle. I wondered for a moment what the strange affliction of this man might be, and whether his obstinate refusal of outside aid was not the result of a rather baseless eccentricity. There is, I reflected tritely, an infinite deal of pathos in the state of an eminent person who has come down in the world.

I might never have known Dr. Muñoz had it not been for the heart attack that suddenly seized me one forenoon as I sat writing in my room. Physicians had told me of the danger of those spells, and I knew there was no time to be lost; so, remembering what the landlady had said about the invalid's help of the injured workman, I dragged myself upstairs and knocked feebly at the door above mine. My knock was answered in good English by a curious voice some distance to the right, asking my name and business; and these things being stated, there came an opening of the door next to the one I had sought.

A rush of cool air greeted me, and though the day was one of the hottest of late June, I shivered as I crossed the threshold into a large apartment whose rich and tasteful decoration surprised me in this nest of squalor and seediness. A folding couch now filled its diurnal role of sofa, and the mahogany furniture, sumptuous hangings, old paintings, and mellow bookshelves all bespoke a gentleman's study rather than a boarding-house bedroom. I now saw that the hall room above mine—the "leetle room" of bottles and machines which Mrs. Herrero had mentioned—was merely the laboratory of the doctor, and that his main living quarters lay in the spacious adjoining room whose convenient alcoves and large contiguous bathroom permitted him to hide all dressers and obtrusively utilitarian devices. Dr. Muñoz, most certainly, was a man of birth, cultivation, and discrimination.

The figure before me was short but exquisitely proportioned, and clad in somewhat formal dress of perfect fit and cut. A high-bred face of masterful though not arrogant expression was adorned by a short iron-gray full beard, and an old-fashioned pince-nez shielded the full, dark eyes and surmounted an aquiline nose which gave a Moorish touch to a physiognomy otherwise dominantly Celtiberian. Thick, well-trimmed hair that argued the punctual calls of a barber was parted gracefully above a high forehead, and the whole picture was one of striking intelligence and superior blood and breeding.

Nevertheless, as I saw Dr. Muñoz in that blast of cool air, I felt a repugnance which nothing in his aspect could justify. Only his lividly inclined complexion and coldness of touch could have afforded a physical basis for this feeling, and even these things should have been excusable considering the man's known invalidism. It might, too, have been the singular cold that alienated me; for such chilliness was abnormal on so hot a day, and the abnormal always excites aversion, distrust, and fear.

But repugnance was soon forgotten in admiration, for the strange physician's extreme skill at once became manifest despite the ice-coldness and shakiness of his bloodless-looking hands. He clearly understood my needs at a glance, and ministered to them with a master's deftness, the while reassuring me in a finely modulated though oddly hollow and timbreless voice that he was the bitterest of sworn enemies to death, and had sunk his fortune and lost all his friends in a lifetime of bizarre experiment devoted to its bafflement and extirpation. Something of the benevolent fanatic seemed to reside in him, and he rambled on almost garrulously as he sounded my chest and mixed a suitable draught of drugs fetched from the smaller laboratory room. Evidently he found the society of a well-born man a rare novelty in this dingy environment, and was moved to unaccustomed speech as memories of better days surged over him.

His voice, if queer, was at least soothing, and I could not even perceive that he breathed as the fluent sentences rolled urbanely out. He sought to distract my mind from my own seizure by speaking of his theories and experiments, and I remember his tactfully consoling me about my heart by insisting that will and consciousness are stronger than organic life itself, so that if a bodily frame be but originally healthy and carefully preserved, it may through a scientific enhancement of these qualities retain a kind of nervous animation despite the most serious impairments, defects, or even absences in the battery of specific organs. He might, he half jestingly said, some day teach me to live—or at least to possess some kind of conscious existence—without any heart at all! For his part, he was afflicted with a complication of maladies requiring a very exact regimen which included constant cold. Any marked rise in temperature might, if prolonged, affect him fatally, and the frigidity of his habitation—some fifty-five or fifty-six degrees Fahrenheit—was maintained by an absorption system of ammonia cooling, the gasoline engine of whose pumps I had often heard in my own room below.

Relieved of my seizure in a marvelously short while, I left the shivery place a disciple and devotee of the gifted recluse. After that I paid him frequent overcoated calls, listening while he told of secret researches and almost ghastly results, and trembling a bit when I examined the unconventional and astonishingly ancient volumes on his shelves. I was eventually, I may add, almost cured of my disease for all time by his skillful ministrations. It seems that he did not scorn the incantations of the medievalists, since he believed these cryptic formulae to contain rare psychological stimuli which might conceivably have singular effects on the substance of a nervous system from which organic pulsations had fled. I was touched by his account of the aged Dr. Torres of Valencia, who had shared his earlier experiments and nursed him through the great illness of eighteen years before, whence his present disorders proceeded. No sooner had the venerable practitioner saved his colleague than he himself succumbed to the grim enemy he had fought. Perhaps the strain had been too great; for Dr. Muñoz made it whisperingly clear—though not in detail—that the methods of healing had been most extraordinary, involving scenes and processes not welcomed by elderly and conservative Galens.

As the weeks passed, I observed with regret that my new

friend was indeed slowly but unmistakably losing ground physically, as Mrs. Herrero had suggested. The livid aspect of his countenance was intensified, his voice became more hollow and indistinct, his muscular motions were less perfectly coordinated, and his mind and will displayed less resilience and initiative. Of this sad change he seemed by no means unaware, and little by little his expression and conversation both took on a gruesome irony which restored in me something of the subtle repulsion I had originally felt.

He developed strange caprices, acquiring a fondness for exotic spices and Egyptian incense till his room smelled like the vault of a sepulchred Pharaoh in the Valley of Kings. At the same time, his demands for cold air increased, and with my aid he amplified the ammonia piping of his room and modified the pumps and feed of his refrigerating machine till he could keep the temperature as low as thirty-four or forty degrees, and finally even twenty-eight degrees; the bathroom and laboratory, of course, being less chilled, in order that water might not freeze, and that chemical processes might not be impeded. The tenant adjoining him complained of the icy air from around the connecting door, so I helped him fit heavy hangings to obviate the difficulty. A kind of growing horror, of outré and morbid cast, seemed to possess him. He talked of death incessantly, but laughed hollowly when such things as burial or funeral arrangements were gently suggested.

All in all, he became a disconcerting and even gruesome companion, yet in my gratitude for his healing, I could not well abandon him to the strangers around him, and was careful to dust his room and attend to his needs each day, muffled in a heavy ulster which I bought especially for the purpose. I likewise did much of his shopping, and gasped in bafflement at some of the chemicals he ordered from druggists and laboratory supply houses.

An increasing and unexplained atmosphere of panic seemed to rise around his apartment. The whole house, as I have said, had a musty odor, but the smell in his room was worse, and in spite of all the spices and incense, and the pungent chemicals of the now incessant baths which he insisted on taking unaided, I perceived that it must be connected with his ailment, and shuddered when I reflected on what that ailment might be. Mrs. Herrero crossed herself when she looked at him, and gave him up unreservedly to me, not even letting her son Esteban continue to run errands for him. When I suggested other physicians, the sufferer would fly into as much of a rage as he seemed to dare to entertain. He evidently feared the physical effect of violent emotion, yet his will and driving force waxed rather than waned, and he refused to be confined to his bed. The lassitude of his earlier ill days gave place to a return of his fiery purpose, so that he seemed about to hurl defiance at the death-demon even as that ancient enemy seized him. The pretence of eating, always curiously like a formality with him, he virtually abandoned, and mental power alone appeared to keep him from total collapse.

He acquired a habit of writing long documents of some sort, which he carefully sealed and filled with injunctions that I transmit them after his death to certain persons whom he named—for the most part lettered East Indians, but including a once celebrated French physician now generally thought dead, and about whom the most inconceivable things had been whispered. As it happened, I burned all these papers undelivered and unopened. His aspect and voice became utterly frightful, and his presence almost unbearable. One September day an unexpected glimpse of him induced an epileptic fit in a man who had come to repair his electric desk lamp, a fit for which he prescribed effectively while keeping himself well out of sight. That man, oddly enough, had been through the terrors of the great war without having incurred any fright so thorough.

Then, in the middle of October, the horror of horrors came with stupefying suddenness. One night about eleven the pump of the refrigerating machine broke down, so that within three hours the process of ammonia cooling became impossible. Dr. Muñoz summoned me by thumping on the floor, and I worked desperately to repair the injury while my host cursed in a tone whose lifeless, rattling hollowness surpassed description. My amateur efforts, however, proved of no use, and when I had brought in a mechanic from a neighboring all-night garage, we learned that nothing could be done until morning, when a new piston would have to be obtained. The moribund hermit's rage and fear, swelling to grotesque proportions, seemed likely to shatter what remained of his failing physique, and once a spasm caused him to clap his hands to his eyes and rush into the bathroom. He groped his way out with face tightly bandaged, and I never saw his eyes again.

The frigidity of the apartment was now sensibly diminishing, and at about five in the morning, the doctor retired to the bathroom, commanding me to keep him supplied with all the ice I could obtain at all-night drugstores and cafeterias. As I would return from my sometimes discouraging trips and lay my spoils before the closed bathroom door, I could hear a restless splashing within, and a thick voice croaking out the order for "More—more!" At length a warm day broke, and the shops opened one by one. I asked Esteban either to help with the ice-fetching while I obtained the pump piston, or to order the piston while I continued with the ice; but, instructed by his mother, he absolutely refused.

Finally I hired a seedy-looking loafer whom I encountered on the corner of Eighth Avenue to keep the patient supplied with ice from a little shop where I introduced him, and applied myself diligently to the task of finding a pump piston and engaging workmen competent to install it. The task seemed interminable, and I raged almost as violently as the hermit when I saw the hours slipping by in a breathless, fruitless round of vain telephoning, and a hectic quest from place to place, hither and thither by subway and surface car. About noon I encountered a suitable supply house far downtown, and at approximately one-thirty that afternoon arrived at my boarding place with the necessary paraphernalia and two sturdy and intelligent mechanics. I had done all I could, and hoped I was in time.

Black terror, however, had preceded me. The house was in utter turmoil, and above the chatter of awed voices I heard a man praying in a deep basso. Fiendish things were in the air, and lodgers told over the beads of their rosaries as they caught the odor from beneath the doctor's closed door. The lounger I had hired, it seems, had fled screaming and mad-eyed not long after his second delivery of ice: perhaps as a result of excessive curiosity. He could not, of course, have locked the door behind him; yet it was now fastened, presumably from the inside. There was no sound within save a nameless sort of slow, thick dripping.

Briefly consulting with Mrs. Herrero and the workmen despite a fear that gnawed my inmost soul, I advised the breaking down of the door, but the landlady found a way to turn the key from the outside with some wire device. We had previously opened the doors of all the other rooms on that hall, and flung all the windows to the very top. Now, noses protected by handkerchiefs, we tremblingly invaded the accursed south room, which blazed with the warm sun of early afternoon.

A kind of dark, slimy trail led from the open bathroom door to the hall door, and thence to the desk, where a terrible little pool had accumulated. Something was scrawled there in pencil in an awful, blind hand on a piece of paper hideously smeared as though by the very claws that traced the hurried last words. Then the trail led to the couch and ended unutterably.

What was, or had been, on the couch I cannot and dare not say here. But this is what I shiveringly puzzled out on the stickily smeared paper before I drew a match and burned it to a crisp; what I puzzled out in terror as the landlady and two mechanics rushed frantically from that hellish place to babble their incoherent stories at the nearest police station. The nauseous words seemed well-nigh incredible in that yellow sunlight, with the clatter of cars and motor trucks ascending clamorously from crowded Fourteenth Street, yet I confess that I believed them then. Whether I believe them now I honestly do not know. There are things about which it is better not to speculate, and all that I can say is that I hate the smell of ammonia, and grow faint at a draught of unusually cool air.

"The end," ran that noisome scrawl, "is here. No more ice—the man looked and ran away. Warmer every minute, and the tissues can't last. I fancy you know—what I said about the will and the nerves and the preserved body after the organs ceased to work. It was good theory, but couldn't keep up indefinitely. There was a gradual deterioration I had not foreseen. Dr. Torres knew, but the shock killed him. He couldn't stand what he had to do; he had to get me in a strange, dark place, when he minded my letter and nursed me back. And the organs never would work again. It had to be done my way—artificial preservation—*for you see I died that time eighteen years ago.*"

Transition

ALGERNON BLACKWOOD

How it happened he never exactly knew. He saw a Monster glaring at him with eyes of blazing fire.

John Mudbury was on his way home from the shops, his arms full of Christmas presents. It was after six o'clock and the streets were very crowded. He was an ordinary man, lived in an ordinary suburban flat, with an ordinary wife and ordinary children. *He* did not think them ordinary, but everybody else did. He had ordinary presents for each one, a cheap blotter for his wife, a cheap air-gun for the boy, and so forth. He was over fifty, bald, in an office, decent in mind and habits, of uncertain opinions, uncertain politics, and uncertain religion. Yet he considered himself a decided, positive gentleman, quite unaware that the morning newspaper determined his opinions for the day. He just lived—from day to day. Physically, he was fit enough, except for a weak heart (which never troubled him); and his summer holiday was bad golf, while the children bathed and his wife read Garvice on the sands. Like the majority of men, he dreamed idly of the past, muddled away the present, and guessed vaguely—after imaginative reading on occasions —at the future.

"I'd like to survive all right," he said, "provided it's better than this," surveying his wife and children, and thinking of his daily toil. "Otherwise—!" and he shrugged his shoulders as a brave man should.

He went to church regularly. But nothing in church convinced him that he did survive, just as nothing in church enticed him into hoping that he would. On the other hand, nothing in life persuaded him that he didn't, wouldn't, couldn't. "I'm an Evolutionist," he loved to say to thoughtful cronies (over a glass), having never heard that Darwinism had been questioned.

And so he came home gaily, happily, with his bunch of Christmas presents "for the wife and little ones," stroking himself upon their keen enjoyment and excitement. The night before he had taken "the wife" to see *Magic* at a select London theatre where the Intellectuals went—and had been extraordinarily stirred. He had gone questioningly, yet expecting something out of the common. "It's *not* musical," he warned her, "nor farce, nor comedy, so to speak"; and in answer to her question as to what the critics had said, he had wriggled, sighed, and put his gaudy necktie straight four times in quick succession. For no Man in the Street, with any claim to self-respect, could be expected to understand what the critics had said, even if he understood the Play. And John had answered truthfully: "Oh, they just said things. But the theatre's always full—and that's the only test."

And just now, as he crossed the crowded Circus to catch his bus, it chanced that his mind (having glimpsed an advertisement) was full of this particular Play, or, rather, of the effect it had produced upon him at the time. For it had thrilled him—inexplicably: with its marvelous speculative hint, its big audacity, its alert and spiritual beauty. . . . Thought plunged to find something—plunged after this bizarre suggestion of a bigger universe, after this quasi-jocular suggestion that man is not the only—then dashed full tilt against a sentence that memory thrust beneath his nose: "Science does *not* exhaust the Universe"—and at the same time dashed full tilt against destruction of another kind as well. . . !

How it happened he never exactly knew. He saw a Monster glaring at him with eyes of blazing fire. It was horrible! It rushed upon him. He dodged. . . . Another Monster met him around the corner. Both came at him simultaneously. He dodged again—a leap that might have cleared a hurdle easily, but was too late. Between the pair of them—his heart literally in his gullet—he was mercilessly caught. Bones crunched. . . . There was a soft sensation, icy cold and hot as fire. Horns and voices roared. Battering rams he saw, and a carapace of iron. . . . Then dazzling light. . . . "Always *face* the traffic!" he remembered with a frantic yell—and, by some extraordinary luck, escaped miraculously onto the opposite pavement.

There was no doubt about it. By the skin of his teeth he had dodged a rather ugly death. First . . . he felt for his presents—all were safe. And then, instead of congratulating himself and taking breath, he hurried homewards—on foot, which proved that his mind had lost control a bit!—thinking only how disappointed the wife and children would have been if—well, if anything had happened. Another thing he realized, oddly enough, was that he no longer really loved his wife, but had only great affection for her. What made him think of that,

Heaven only knows, but he *did* think of it. He was an honest man without pretence. This came as a discovery somehow. He turned a moment, and saw the crowd gathered about the entangled taxicabs, policemen's helmets gleaming in the lights of the shop windows . . . then hurried on again, his thoughts full of the joy his presents would give . . . of the scampering children . . . and of his wife—bless her silly heart!—eyeing the mysterious parcels. . . .

And, though he never could explain how, he presently stood at the foot of the jail-like building that contained his flat, having walked the whole three miles. His thoughts had been so busy and absorbed that he had hardly noticed the length of weary trudge. "Besides," he reflected, thinking of the narrow escape, "I've had a nasty shock. It was a d———d near thing, now I come to think of it. . . ." He still felt a bit shaky and bewildered. Yet, at the same time, he felt extraordinarily jolly and lighthearted.

He counted his Christmas parcels . . . hugged himself in anticipatory joy . . . and let himself in swiftly with his latch-key. "I'm late," he realized, "but when she sees the brown paper parcels, she'll forget to say a word. God bless the old faithful soul." And he softly used the key a second time and entered his flat on tiptoe. . . . In his mind was the master impulse of that afternoon—the pleasure these Christmas presents would give his wife and children.

He heard a noise. He hung up hat and coat in the poky vestibule (they never called it "hall") and moved softly towards the parlor door, holding the packages behind him. Only of them he thought, not of himself—of his family, that is, not of the packages. Pushing the door cunningly ajar, he peeped in shyly. To his amazement the room was full of people. He withdrew quickly, wondering what it meant. A party? And without his knowing about it! Extraordinary! . . . Keen disappointment came over him. But as he stepped back, the vestibule, he saw, was full of people too. . . .

He was uncommonly surprised, yet somehow not surprised at all. People were congratulating him. There was a perfect mob of them. Moreover, he knew them all—vaguely remembered them, at least. And they all knew him.

"Isn't it a game?" laughed someone, patting him on the back. "*They* haven't the least idea . . .!"

And the speaker—it was old John Palmer, the bookkeeper at the office—emphasized the "they."

"Not the least idea," he answered with a smile, saying something he didn't understand, yet knew was right.

His face, apparently, showed the utter bewilderment he felt. The shock of the collision had been greater than he realized evidently. His mind was wandering. . . . Possibly! Only the odd thing was—he had never felt so clearheaded in his life. Ten thousand things grew simple suddenly. But, how thickly these people pressed about him, and how—familiarly!

"My parcels," he said, joyously pushing his way across the throng. "These are Christmas presents I've bought for them." He nodded toward the room. "I've saved for weeks—stopped cigars and billiards and—and several other good things—to buy them."

"Good man!" said Palmer with a happy laugh. "It's the heart that counts."

Mudbury looked at him. Palmer had said an amazing truth, only—people would hardly understand and believe him. . . . Would they?

"Eh?" he asked, feeling stuffed and stupid, muddled somewhere between two meanings, one of which was gorgeous and other stupid beyond belief.

"If you *please,* Mr. Mudbury, step inside. They are expecting you," said a kindly, pompous voice. And, turning sharply, he met the gentle, foolish eyes of Sir James Epiphany, a director of the Bank where he worked.

The effect of the voice was instantaneous from long habit.

"They are." He smiled from his heart, and advanced as from the custom of many years. Oh, how happy and gay he felt! His affection for his wife was real. Romance, indeed, had gone, but he needed her—and she needed him. And the children—Milly, Bill, and Jean—he deeply loved them. Life was worth living indeed!

In the room was a crowd, but—an astounding silence. John Mudbury looked around him. He advanced towards his wife, who sat in the corner armchair with Milly on her knee. A lot of people talked and moved about. Momentarily the crowd increased. He stood in front of them—in front of Milly and his wife. And he spoke—holding out his packages. "It's Christmas Eve," he whispered shyly, "and I've—brought you something—something for everybody. Look!" He held the packages before their eyes.

"Of course, of course," said a voice behind him, "but you may hold them out like that for a century. They'll *never* see them!"

"Of course they won't. But I love to do the old, sweet thing," replied John Mudbury—then wondered with a gasp of stark amazement why he said it.

"*I* think—" whispered Milly, staring around her.

"Well, what *do* you think?" her mother asked sharply. "You're always thinking something queer."

"I think," the girl continued dreamily, "that Daddy's already here." She paused, then added with a child's impossible conviction, "I'm sure he is. I *feel* him."

There was an extraordinary laugh. Sir James Epiphany laughed. The others—the whole crowd of them—also turned their heads and smiled. But the mother, thrusting the child away from her, rose up suddenly with a violent start. Her face had turned to chalk. She stretched her arms out—into the air before her. She gasped and shivered. There was anguish in her eyes.

"Look!" repeated John, "these are the presents that I brought."

But his voice apparently was soundless. And, with a spasm of icy pain, he remembered that Palmer and Sir James—some years ago—had died.

"It's magic," he cried, "but—I love you, Jinny—I love you—and—and I have always been true to you—as true as steel. We need each other—oh, can't you see—we go on together—you and I—for ever and ever—"

"*Think,*" interrupted an exquisitely tender voice, "don't shout! They can't *hear* you—now." And, turning, John Mudbury met the eyes of Everard Minturn, their President of the year before. Minturn had gone down with the *Titanic.*

He dropped his parcels then. His heart gave an enormous leap of joy.

He saw her face—the face of his wife—look through him.

But the child gazed straight into his eyes. She *saw* him.

The next thing he knew was that he heard something tinkling . . . far, far away. It sounded miles below him—inside him—he was sounding himself—all utterly bewildering—like a bell. It *was* a bell.

Milly stooped down and picked the parcels up. Her face shone with happiness and laughter. . . .

But a man came in soon after, a man with a ridiculous, solemn face, a pencil and a notebook. He wore a dark-blue helmet. Behind him came a string of other men. They carried something . . . something . . . he could not see exactly what it was. But, when he pressed forward through the laughing throng to gaze upon it, he dimly made out two eyes, a nose, a chin, a deep red smear, and a pair of folded hands upon an overcoat. A woman's form fell down upon them then, and he heard soft sounds of children weeping strangely . . . and other sounds . . . as of familiar voices laughing . . . laughing gaily.

"They'll join us presently. It goes like a flash . . ."

And, turning with great happiness in his heart, he saw that Sir James had said it, holding Palmer by the arm as with some natural yet unexpected love of sympathetic friendship.

"Come on," said Palmer, smiling like a man who accepts a gift in universal fellowship, "let's help 'em. They'll never understand. . . . Still, we can always try."

The entire throng moved up with laughter and amusement. It was a moment of hearty, genuine life at last. Delight and Joy and Peace were everywhere.

Then John Mudbury realized the truth—that he was dead.

Housebound

R. CHETWYND-HAYES

The urge to summon that vile creature in the woodwork was nigh irresistible.

He, if indeed that which remained of Charlie Wheatland could be designated as "he," was most happy when he was in the woodwork. The wainscoting, the picture rails, the large wardrobe, the dressing-table, and sometimes the floorboards; the coarse-grained pine, the tough oak, enabled him to spread out, to become as water on blotting paper, to dim down his never-sleeping consciousness to a gentle twilight. The walls were not so kind, the bricks and plaster did not absorb him so easily, and the thoughts of the room's occupants clung to the faded wallpaper like flies on a hot day.

A certain measure of peace was to be found during the

daylight hours when the bedroom was empty, and he could roll out across the woodwork in soft invisible waves and not be disturbed by the mental vibrations of living people. The man did not disturb him much, although his harsh passions sometimes seared Charlie's consciousness like a white-hot knife.

But the woman was a magnet that drew him towards her and some form of grotesque life. Charlie hated and feared her; the powerful raw power reached out tentacles that found him no matter where he might hide. Like a mouse chased by a cat he fled before them, sometimes drawing himself up into a tight ball, at others spreading himself over every square inch of room and furniture, quelling the urge to submit and allow the power to make of him what it would. "I want to be nothing," the sobbing cry sometimes made itself heard in the form of a deep sigh, and the woman would pause in the midst of bed-making and look fearfully over one shoulder. "I want to forget, to sleep—to sleep."

"Surely you know," said Mrs. Hardcastle, sipping her tea in a most ladylike fashion, "I mean the estate agent should have told you before actually selling you the house."

"Not a word." Celia Cooper breathed deeply and wondered when the woman would leave. She knew that her visitor's bright little eyes were valuing the furniture to the exact penny, and mentally noting her personal defects as to dress and hair style. "You see we were so pleased to get finally settled—you know what it's like trying to find a decent house at a reasonable price?"

"Do I not, dear!" Mrs. Hardcastle waved her free hand and with practiced skill balanced the tea cup with the other. "The trouble Arthur and I had before we found 'Quiet Haven'! But, all said and done, the man *should* have told you."

"What *is* the story?" Celia did her best to sound interested, but she could imagine what was coming. A previous tenant who had loved well but unwisely; an outwardly respectable clerk who had absconded with the contents of his employer's safe; or perhaps something more sordid. She had long since discovered that the sins and misfortunes of the few give much joy to the many.

"My dear," Mrs. Hardcastle's eyes shone with pleasurable horror, "a man was shot dead in this house, in your front bedroom."

Celia Cooper did not move, refused to allow a single muscle to betray her, but the naked fear was now out in the open. She said calmly:

"How terrible. Was it—murder?"

"Not exactly. It all happened ten years ago, just after this estate was built. I'm surprised you don't remember the details, they were in all the newspapers."

"You forget"—Celia managed to smile—"until last month Harold and I had not set foot in England for fifteen years."

"Of course." Mrs. Hardcastle tittered behind her hand. "How silly of me . . . Well, he was a little crook, the man that was shot, I mean, called Charlie Wheatland, and he held up the bank in the High Street. He shot a clerk who managed to push the alarm button or whatever it is they do push, and made his getaway chased by a police car. They finally got him pinned down in this road, and he took cover in this very house, which was empty, as the builders had only moved out the previous day. There was a terrific gun battle which lasted for hours, until a police marksman got a bead on him from the house opposite. They found him in your front bedroom with a hole in his head. . . . My dear, you've gone quite pale. I shouldn't have told you, but really, I did think you ought to know."

"Please don't mind me." Celia smiled again. "But it *is* rather a shock to find out your house was once the scene of a violent death. I gather this notoriety did not stop the house being sold—I mean it hasn't stood empty these past ten years?"

"Good heavens, no." Mrs. Hardcastle put down her cup and started to pull on a pair of black lace gloves. "Mr. and Mrs. Dowsett lived here until Mr. Dowsett was killed in a motor accident. Mind you, Jane did say to me on one occasion she never really felt happy in that front bedroom. But that's to be expected, I mean when one knows what happened there. . . . Oh, how tactless of me, I do hope you won't . . ."

"I won't give it another thought," lied Celia. "I have no time to spare to worry about ghosts. Must you leave so soon, it has been nice meeting you. . . ."

"Harold," Celia looked at her husband seated on the other side of the dining-room table, "did you know a man had been shot dead in this house?"

Harold Cooper put down his soup spoon and watched his wife with an appreciative eye as she took the plates of roast lamb from the heated food trolley. "Yes, I knew. The chap at the estate agents told me when I bought the place. I didn't see any point in telling you. It might have put you off, and I believe that what the ear doesn't hear, the mind doesn't worry over. Who told you?"

"A neighbor, a Mrs. Hardcastle. She paid me a visit this afternoon, superficially to make my acquaintance, but in reality I suspect to see what we had, and estimate its cost."

"Big-mouthed old hussy," Harold grunted. "Well, now you know. I shouldn't let it worry you. Someone was bound to die in the house sooner or later; we shall probably die here ourselves one day. The manner of dying isn't all that important, the main thing is the little rat *did* die. It's a pity a lot more of his kind don't come to the same end. Shoot the lot, I say. There's too much molly-coddling of these young thugs."

Celia said: "Yes, dear, you have mentioned the matter on various occasions," and then steered the conversation into more mundane channels until the time came for her to clear the table and wash up in the stainless-steel and formica-panelled kitchen. When she had finished her work and hung the wiping-up towel on the telescopic towel rail, she returned to the living-room and found Harold watching television—but not, she noted, with any great interest, for his head was already drooping and it would not be long before he was prone in his seat with fast-closed eyes and gaping mouth. Celia turned off the set and took up a book, and every once in a while glanced at her sleeping husband. After twenty-five years of married life together she knew him as well as any one human being knows another; if she were attacked by a gang of thugs, he would fight to defend her, even to the sacrifice of his life; if she were in some sort of trouble, no matter how dreadful, he would help her, for Harold was, above all, a husband, and she was his wife.

But supposing she were threatened by a danger inconceivable to his practical turn of mind; if she were now to wake him and cry: "There is a—something in our bedroom—something horrible, wicked and pathetic, that torments me, floods my mind with unspeakable horror, fascinates me. *Please* let us move away from here." He would, after the initial surprise, talk of tonics, rundown, "pop along and see the old quack," and if she persisted, his thin lips would set in a straight obstinate line, and he would point out that this was a good house in a nice neighborhood, it suited him, he had done a lot of work on it, and be damned if he was going to move because of her hysteria and imagination. His unimaginative logic would become an iron wall, and if she continued to fight him, something vital in their marriage would die, to be replaced by fear, mistrust and finally hatred. This was one battle she must fight by herself, try to decide what was fact and how much of this terror was due to imagination. Of late Celia had come to believe that there was no such thing as imagination, only fact viewed from different angles; what was life but a series of colored lights reflected on a white screen?

"Harold," she called softly, "wake up."

"What's the matter?" He started and blinked foolishly, looking like a gray-haired schoolboy. "Must have dozed off."

"You'll never sleep tonight." She smiled indulgently. "Would you like a hot drink?"

"If you like." He yawned as she rose and went into the kitchen.

She lay beside Harold in the large double bed and listened to the even tempo of his breathing. He slept so deeply, encased in a cocoon of unconsciousness from which it would take five minutes of shaking to rouse him. She tried to keep her thoughts under control and not to let them wander around the darkened room, seeking, prodding, even as a mischievous child might goad a sleeping snake, aware of the danger, but drawn to that danger, like a moth who must fly into a lighted candle.

He had spread himself out, along the wainscoting, over the wardrobe, into the dressing-table; a thin layer of whimpering, hate-streaked fear. Without being aware that she had exerted any effort, Celia found she had driven him out of the dressing-table, made him retreat from the wardrobe; now he flowed up the walls; she knew he hated the walls and pursued him relentlessly, and all the while her body shook with sickening horror. Now came the climax; she must change her tactics, draw him towards the bed and make him become a ball of pulsating life. He came, fighting every inch of the way; but he came. The walls and the woodwork were free, and he was there, on the floor at the foot of the bed. Celia shivered with intense cold as the power drained out of her, but there was no going back; whatever it was that crouched on the floor mingled with the life force that flowed from her body and grew into something tangible, rising slowly into view. The window curtains were drawn back and the top sash was open, for Harold insisted that fresh air was essential in a bedroom, allowing the street lamp to light the room with a soft radiance. He was a black shadow that bore a rough resemblance to a masculine shape; the shoulders appeared to be bowed, a kind of oafish slouch, and Celia thought she could define the pale outlines of a face, but that may have been due to imagination. A whisper came to her, or so she at the time believed, although afterwards it seemed more likely that she translated some mental communication into sound.

"What do you want of me?"

It was then that Celia Cooper came face to face with truth; it came hand-in-hand with knowledge and stood beside the black shadow, and of the two truth was the more fearful. "*What do you want of me*?" She knew why she had summoned this thing from the woodwork, why week after week she had developed the power, which until they had moved into this house she did not suspect she possessed. Celia Cooper, the placid, commonplace housewife of fifty, was akin to Charlie Wheatland, who had died in this room ten years ago. At that moment she could only think of the man who slept by her side; could only remember the dreadful boring years, his selfishness, his lack of imagination, his exasperating commonsense; the fact that she had never consciously realized the extent of these shortcomings before, or knew how much she despised—even hated him—for them, made this moment all the more terrifying. Truth was relentless, more exciting. It was as though she had been blind from birth and now saw for the first time. The fear dropped away like a dark heavy mantle, and a great sense of power flooded her being. Sitting up in bed she pointed to the sleeping form of her husband and cried in a loud voice:

"Kill him, make him as *you* are—kill him."

The figure moved slowly around the bed, grew more tangible until Celia could have sworn a living man was preparing to obey her command; then she saw the white little face, the blazing black eyes, and screamed with renewed terror:

"No, I didn't mean it!"

The figure stopped, turned his face to her, then disintegrated. Celia collapsed back onto her pillow and knew no more until the alarm roused her in the morning.

No one can say he or she is good or virtuous until they have been made to face temptation and found the strength to resist. Celia Cooper had never been tempted before; having always been blessed with sufficient money for her simple needs, there was no temptation to steal, and murder was a crime committed by depraved creatures who were beyond a middle-class housewife's comprehension. This was still true; Celia could no more have physically murdered her husband than she could have set fire to her own house. But this was different, murder by necromancy was not by the laws of the realm murder at all. Celia fought her temptation; it was a battle that raged minute by minute, hour by hour, day by day, and—worst of all—night by night. As she lay beside the sleep-drunk Harold the urge to summon that vile creature in the woodwork was nigh irresistible. The knowledge that it would obey her will overcame the loathing and terror, and made her realize in full her hatred for Harold, which once it had revealed itself grew rather than diminished as time passed.

Celia could feel her character changing in the same way a

man who has contracted a fatal disease can watch his body disintegrating; she could do nothing to slow down the process, let alone kill it. She toyed with the idea of running away; but where would she go, what could she do at her time of life? She had neither the ability nor the urge to earn her own living, whereas if Harold were to suddenly die she would find herself in very easy circumstances. His life was insured for a considerable sum, and despite their simple mode of living he had a respectable fortune in gilt-edged securities; there was also the widow's pension that the oil company for whom he had worked for over thirty years would pay her. Once this unwanted spouse was safely in the grave she could move far away and live under a golden umbrella.

Perhaps she might have successfully fought her battle, if not forever—at least for a long time, had she not one afternoon walked into the bedroom and found Charlie Wheatland fully materialized and standing by the window. So accustomed had she grown to living with this horror, she felt no fear, only surprise as to how he came to be there. She had not consciously summoned him, and could only suppose that having once been called up he had waxed strong on his own account, or fed surreptitiously on her power, possibly while she slept. He turned slowly, his white face a mask of fear and hate, then whispered:

"When?"

Celia stood perfectly still and tried to absorb the knowledge that her eyes witnessed, and at the same time come to terms with the warning bells that were ringing in her brain. Would she be able to control this creature? If he was capable of murdering Harold, what of her? The apparition answered her unspoken question.

"You give me strength. Without you I have no substance."

"But," Celia's thoughts were cold as steel, "suppose Harold were to . . . linger?"

Charlie Wheatland's lips did not move but the words came in a low, distinctive whisper.

"Only bad men are housebound."

"But what of *me*," Celia asked the all-important question, "when *my* time comes . . . ?"

There was a suggestion of a smile on the white face. "Can you not repent—afterwards?"

The last barrier collapsed and Celia breathed a deep sigh of relief; she surrendered completely to the great temptation that had dominated her for weeks, now she could face truth without flinching. Murder could be committed without fear of detection; she wondered how Harold's death would appear; heart failure, possibly, and there need be no price to pay. As the phantom said, she could always repent afterwards.

"Tonight." She thought the answer to his first question. "Must I be present?"

"No." The black eyes glittered with a joyful light. "But you must order me *to* it."

"I order you to kill my husband."

"No, I cannot kill, only free your husband from his body. Order me to free your husband from his body."

"I order you to free my husband from his body."

Something essential went out of Celia as her mind formed these last words; she would have retained it if that had been possible, but it was too late, the fatal step had been taken, and now she stood face to face with her familiar, and knew that repentance was but a word; she must accept this new world where evil reigned supreme. There was pride in her voice when she said aloud:

"I will send him to you this evening."

She went out, closing the bedroom door behind her.

The evening passed much the same as twenty-five years of evenings had passed, only this was the last one. Celia watched Harold eat his steak and kidney pie, served him the cottage pudding he liked so much, then washed up and put the dishes away neatly in the built-in dresser, and all the time she could feel the presence of the thing that lurked in the bedroom. Was it still standing by the window, the very window where its body had been destroyed ten years ago? Or was it resting in the woodwork, waiting for her summons; waiting for Harold to walk into the room?

Harold was sleeping in front of the television, his usual evening prelude to the nightly feast of sleeping; soon he would wallow in sleep; not the snorting, gasping sleep that had so often disturbed her rest, but a dignified cold repose that all the alarm clocks in the world would never break.

The hands of the clock slowly made their endless journey round the white dial; the television relayed its canned trivial entertainment, until Celia turned it off. Her hand was gentle as it shook Harold's shoulder, and her voice was that of a kind, indulgent mother.

"Harold, it's time for bed, wake up or you'll never sleep tonight."

"Wassat!" He opened his eyes, blinked and looked at the clock. "Ten o'clock, must have dozed off."

She made the cocoa and sat opposite as he sipped from his cup, talking of what he must do tomorrow, but his words made little impression upon her. She could feel the thing stirring in the room above.

"Time for beddy-bys." He rose, stretched, then yawned. "Coming, old girl?"

"In a moment. You go up, I'll be with you in a moment."

"Right." He walked heavily from the room. "Don't be long, must be up bright and early tomorrow."

As he left the room she wanted to cry out, to take him by the hand and run from this house, never to return, but even as her mouth opened she felt the power drain out of her. She sank into a chair, unable to speak or move a muscle; the thing upstairs was building himself up, gathering strength for the supreme effort. She heard Harold climbing the stairs; he went into the bathroom and after a lapse of time pulled the lavatory chain, there was a roar of cascading water, then he crossed the landing and opened the bedroom door.

"Forgive me, God, forgive me," Celia was praying in a loud whisper, tears streaming down her face, "forgive me, don't let it happen. . . ."

A loud scream pinned her back against the chair; a cry of indescribable terror, followed by a crash that made the ceiling lamp swing gently from side to side, and light danced with shadows in a mad frenzy of horror. The power flowed back into her limbs, and Celia knew Charlie Wheatland no longer needed her strength; perhaps, this one terrible deed performed, he was now free to descend into the hell from which he had so long been detained, or possibly he was now in some limbo where time and human values were without meaning. Whatever the reason, she could not feel his presence either in the room above or in any part of the house. She sat motionless, trying to accept the fact that Harold lay dead on the bedroom floor, killed by terror and his wife's mad, unsuspected hatred. She could not move, had not the strength or courage to ascend the stairs, only sit and realize that from now onwards she belonged to the damned.

The clock in the hall broke the silence by striking two, and as though this were a signal, Celia heard a sound from the bedroom above. The creak of a loose floorboard, the slightly louder sound of a heavy body climbing to its feet, then a slow tread crossing the carpeted room; slippered feet moving out onto the landing; a bannister groaning its protest when a hand pressed upon it, a loose stair-rod rattling; a terrible harsh breathing growing louder by the second; Celia knew Harold was coming down. At first she experienced a sense of great relief, he was not dead, she was not a murderess; then she realized the foot treads were not Harold's; the harsh breathing was that of a man who has not breathed for a long time; whatever, whoever was coming down the stairs, it was not Harold.

She could not tear her eyes away from the closed door, for surely approaching it from the other side was a horror that rightfully belonged to some dark valley in Hades, and it was coming in to her. She tried to scream when the door handle turned, for to scream would let out some of the icy fear, but the vocal cords froze and no sound came; she clawed at the chair arms as the door swung slowly open, then became still as a corpse, only her eyes and ears continued to function. The body was Harold's, his face dead white, his arms hanging loosely; but the eyes burned with blazing hate, and the labored breathing turned into rasping speech as he approached the armchair.

"Why couldn't you leave me alone—there was peace in the woodwork—peace. . . ."

She found her voice and screamed once as the thing moved in, its arms outstretched.

Contents of the Dead Man's Pocket

JACK FINNEY

There were three letters in his pocket and he lighted each of them, holding each till the flame touched his hand.

At the little living-room desk Tom Benecke rolled two sheets of flimsy and a heavier top sheet, carbon paper sandwiched between them, into his portable. *Inter-office Memo,* the top sheet was headed, and he typed tomorrow's date just below this; then he glanced at a creased yellow sheet, covered with his own handwriting, beside the typewriter. "Hot in here," he muttered to himself. Then from the short hallway at his back he heard the muffled clang of wire coat hangers in the bedroom closet, and at this reminder of what his wife was doing he thought: Hot, hell—guilty conscience.

He got up, shoving his hands into the back pockets of his

gray wash slacks, stepped to the living-room window beside the desk and stood breathing on the glass, watching the expanding circlet of mist, staring down through the autumn night at Lexington Avenue, eleven stories below. He was a tall, lean, dark-haired young man in a pullover sweater, who looked as though he had played not football, probably, but basketball in college. Now he placed the heels of his hands against the top edge of the lower window frame and shoved upwards. But as usual the window didn't budge, and he had to lower his hands and then shoot them hard upwards to jolt the window open a few inches. He dusted his hands, muttering.

But still he didn't begin his work. He crossed the room to the hallway entrance and, leaning against the doorjamb, hands shoved into his back pockets again, he called, "Clare?" When his wife answered, he said, "Sure you don't mind going alone?"

"No." Her voice was muffled, and he knew her head and shoulders were in the bedroom closet. Then the tap of her high heels sounded on the wood floor, and she appeared at the end of the little hallway, wearing a slip, both hands raised to one ear, clipping on an earring. She smiled at him—a slender, very pretty girl with light brown, almost blond, hair—her prettiness emphasized by the pleasant nature that showed in her face. "It's just that I hate you to miss this movie; you wanted to see it, too."

"Yeah, I know." He ran his fingers through his hair. "Got to get this done, though."

She nodded, accepting this. Then, glancing at the desk across the living room, she said, "You work too much, though, Tom—and too hard."

He smiled. "You won't mind, though, will you, when the money comes rolling in and I'm known as the Boy Wizard of Wholesale Groceries?"

"I guess not." She smiled and turned back towards the bedroom.

At his desk again, Tom lighted a cigarette; then a few moments later, as Clare appeared dressed and ready to leave, he set it on the rim of the ashtray. "Just after seven," she said. "I can make the beginning of the first feature."

He walked to the front-door closet to help her on with her coat. He kissed her then and, for an instant, holding her close, smelling the perfume she had used, he was tempted to go with her; it was not actually true that he had to work tonight, though he very much wanted to. This was his own project, unannounced as yet in his office, and it could be postponed. But then they won't see it till Monday, he thought once again, and if I give it to the boss tomorrow he might read it over the weekend. . . . "Have a good time," he said aloud. He gave his wife a little swat and opened the door for her, feeling the air from the building hallway, smelling faintly of floor wax, stream gently past his face.

He watched her walk down the hall, flicked a hand in response as she waved, and then he started to close the door, but it resisted for a moment. As the door opening narrowed, the current of warm air from the hallway, channelled through this smaller opening now, suddenly rushed past him with accelerated force. Behind him he heard the slap of the window curtains against the wall and the sound of paper fluttering from his desk, and he had to push to close the door.

Turning, he saw a sheet of white paper drifting to the floor in a series of arcs, and another sheet, yellow, moving towards the window, caught in the dying current flowing through the narrow opening. As he watched, the paper struck the bottom edge of the window and hung there for an instant, plastered against the glass and wood. Then as the moving air stilled completely, the curtains swinging back from the wall to hang free again, he saw the yellow sheet drop to the window ledge and slide over out of sight.

He ran across the room, grasped the bottom of the window and tugged, staring through the glass. He saw the yellow sheet, dimly now in the darkness outside, lying on the ornamental ledge a yard below the window. Even as he watched, it was moving, scraping slowly along the ledge, pushed by the breeze that pressed steadily against the building wall. He heaved on the window with all his strength, and it shot open with a bang, the window weight rattling in the casing. But the paper was past his reach and, leaning out into the night, he watched it scud steadily along the ledge to the south, half plastered against the building wall. Above the muffled sound of the street traffic far below, he could hear the dry scrape of its movement, like a leaf on the pavement.

The living room of the next apartment to the south projected a yard or more farther out towards the street than this one; because of this the Beneckes paid seven and a half dollars less rent than their neighbors. And now the yellow sheet, sliding along the stone ledge, nearly invisible in the night, was stopped by the projecting blank wall of the next apartment. It lay motionless then, in the corner formed by the two walls a good five yards away, pressed firmly against the ornate corner ornament of the ledge by the breeze that moved past Tom Benecke's face.

He knelt at the window and stared at the yellow paper for a full minute or more, waiting for it to move, to slide off the ledge and fall, hoping he could follow its course to the street, and then hurry down in the elevator and retrieve it. But it didn't move, and then he saw that the paper was caught firmly between a projection of the convoluted corner ornament and the ledge. He thought about the poker from the fireplace, then the broom, then the mop—discarding each thought as it occurred to him. There was nothing in the apartment long enough to reach that paper.

It was hard for him to understand that he actually had to abandon it—it was ridiculous—and he began to curse. Of all the papers on his desk, why did it have to be this one in particular! On four long Saturday afternoons he had stood in supermarkets, counting the people who passed certain displays, and the results were scribbled on that yellow sheet. From stacks of trade publications, gone over page by page in snatched half hours at work and during evenings at home, he had copied facts, quotations, and figures onto that sheet. And he had carried it with him to the Public Library on Fifth Avenue, where he'd spent a dozen lunch hours and early evenings adding more. All were needed to support and lend authority to his idea for a new grocery-store display method; without them his idea was a mere opinion. And there they all lay, in his own improvised shorthand—countless hours of work—out there on the ledge.

For many seconds he believed he was going to abandon the yellow sheet, that there was nothing else to do. The work could be duplicated. But it would take two months, and the time to present this idea, damn it, was *now,* for use in the spring displays. He struck his fist on the window ledge. Then he shrugged. Even though his plan was adopted, he told himself, it wouldn't bring him a raise in pay—not immediately, anyway, or as a direct result. It won't bring me a promotion either, he argued—not of itself.

But just the same, and he couldn't escape the thought, this and other independent projects, some already done and others planned for the future, would gradually mark him out from the score of other young men in his company. They were the way to change from a name on the payroll to a name in the minds of the company officials. They were the beginning of the long, long climb to where he was determined to be—at the very top. And he knew he was going out there in the darkness, after the yellow sheet fifteen feet beyond his reach.

By a kind of instinct, he instantly began making his intention acceptable to himself by laughing at it. The mental picture of himself sidling along the ledge outside was absurd—it was actually comical—and he smiled. He imagined himself describing it; it would make a good story at the office and, it occurred to him, would add a special interest and importance to his memorandum, which would do it no harm at all.

To simply go out and get his paper was an easy task—he could be back here with it in less than two minutes—and he knew he wasn't deceiving himself. The ledge, he saw, measuring it with his eye, was about as wide as the length of his shoe, and perfectly flat. And every fifth row of brick in the face of the building, he remembered—leaning out, he verified this—was indented half an inch, enough for the tips of his fingers, enough to maintain balance easily. It occurred to him that if this ledge and wall were only a yard above ground—as he knelt at the window staring out, this thought was the final confirmation of his intention—he could move along the ledge indefinitely.

On a sudden impulse, he got to his feet, walked to the front closet and took out an old tweed jacket; it would be cold outside. He put it on and buttoned it as he crossed the room rapidly towards the open window. In the back of his mind he knew he'd better hurry and get this over with before he thought too much, and at the window he didn't allow himself to hesitate.

He swung a leg over the sill, then felt for and found the ledge a yard below the window with his foot. Gripping the bottom of the window frame very tightly and carefully, he slowly ducked his head under it, feeling on his face the sudden change from the warm air of the room to the chill outside. With infinite care he brought out his other leg, his mind concentrating on what he was doing. Then he slowly stood erect. Most of the putty, dried out and brittle, had dropped off the bottom edging of the window frame, he found, and the flat wooden edging provided a good gripping surface, a half inch or more deep, for the tips of his fingers.

Now, balanced easily and firmly, he stood on the ledge outside in the slight, chill breeze, eleven stories above the street, staring into his own lighted apartment, odd and different-seeming now.

First his right hand, then his left, he carefully shifted his finger-tip grip from the puttyless window edging to an indented row of bricks directly to his right. It was hard to take the first shuffling sideways step then—to make himself move—and the fear stirred in his stomach, but he did it, again by not allowing himself time to think. And now—with his chest, stomach, and the left side of his face pressed against the rough cold brick—his lighted apartment was suddenly gone, and it was much darker out here than he had thought.

Without pause he continued—right foot, left foot, right foot, left—his shoe soles shuffling and scraping along the rough stone, never lifting from it, fingers sliding along the exposed edging of brick. He moved on the balls of his feet, heels lifted slightly; the ledge was not quite as wide as he'd expected. But leaning slightly inward towards the face of the building and pressed against it, he could feel his balance firm and secure, and moving along the ledge was quite as easy as he had thought it would be. He could hear the buttons of his jacket scraping steadily along the rough bricks and feel them catch momentarily, tugging a little, at each mortared crack. He simply did not permit himself to look down, though the compulsion to do so never left him; nor did he allow himself actually to think. Mechanically—right foot, left foot, over and again—he shuffled along crabwise, watching the projecting wall ahead loom steadily closer. . . .

Then he reached it and, at the corner—he'd decided how he was going to pick up the paper—he lifted his right foot and placed it carefully on the ledge that ran along the projecting wall at a right angle to the ledge on which his other foot rested. And now, facing the building, he stood in the corner formed by the two walls, one foot on the ledging of each, a hand on the shoulder-high indentation of each wall. His forehead was pressed directly into the corner against the cold bricks, and now he carefully lowered first one hand, then the other, perhaps a foot farther down, to the next indentation in the rows of bricks.

Very slowly, sliding his forehead down the trough of the brick corner and bending his knees, he lowered his body towards the paper lying between his outstretched feet. Again he lowered his fingerholds another foot and bent his knees still more, thigh muscles taut, his forehead sliding and bumping down the brick V. Half squatting now, he dropped his left hand to the next indentation and then slowly reached with his right hand towards the paper between his feet.

He couldn't quite touch it, and his knees now were pressed against the wall; he could bend them no farther. But by ducking his head another inch lower, the top of his head now pressed against the bricks, he lowered his right shoulder and his fingers had the paper by a corner, pulling it loose. At the same instant he saw, between his legs and far below, Lexington Avenue stretched out for miles ahead.

He saw, in that instant, the Loew's theatre sign, blocks ahead past Fiftieth Street; the miles of traffic signals, all green now; the lights of cars and street lamps; countless neon signs; and the moving black dots of people. And a violent, instantaneous explosion of absolute terror roared through him. For a motionless instant he saw himself externally—bent practically double, balanced on this narrow ledge, nearly half his body projecting out above the street far below—and he began to tremble violently, panic flaring through his mind and muscles, and he felt the blood rush from the surface of his skin.

In the fractional moment before horror paralyzed him, as he stared between his legs at that terrible length of street far beneath him, a fragment of his mind raised his body in a spasmodic jerk to an upright position again, but so violently that his head scraped hard against the wall, bouncing off it, and his body swayed outwards to the knife edge of balance, and he very nearly plunged backwards and fell. Then he was leaning far into the corner again, squeezing and pushing into it, not only his face but his chest and stomach, his back arching; and his finger tips clung with all the pressure of his pulling arms to the shoulder-high half-inch indentation in the bricks.

He was more than trembling now; his whole body was racked with a violent shuddering beyond control, his eyes squeezed so tightly shut it was painful, though he was past awareness of that. His teeth were exposed in a frozen grimace, the strength draining like water from his knees and calves. It was extremely likely, he knew, that he would faint, slump down along the wall, his face scraping, and then drop backwards, a limp weight, out into nothing. And to save his life he concentrated on holding on to consciousness, drawing deliberate deep breaths of cold air into his lungs, fighting to keep his senses aware.

Then he knew that he would not faint, but he could not stop shaking nor open his eyes. He stood where he was, breathing deeply, trying to hold back the terror of the glimpse he had had of what lay below him; and he knew he had made a mistake in not making himself stare down at the street, getting used to it and accepting it, when he had first stepped out onto the ledge.

It was impossible to walk back. He simply could not do it. He couldn't bring himself to make the slightest movement. The strength was gone from his legs; his shivering hands—numb, cold, and desperately rigid—had lost all deftness; his easy ability to move and balance was gone. Within a step or two, if he tried to move, he knew that he would stumble clumsily and fall.

Seconds passed, with the chill faint wind pressing the side of his face, and he could hear the toned-down volume of the street traffic far beneath him. Again and again it slowed and then stopped, almost to silence; then presently, even this high, he would hear the click of the traffic signals and the subdued roar of the cars starting up again. During a lull in the street sounds, he called out. Then he was shouting "*Help*!" so loudly it rasped his throat. But he felt the steady pressure of the wind, moving between his face and the blank wall, snatch up his cries as he uttered them, and he knew they must sound directionless and distant. And he remembered how habitually, here in New York, he himself heard and ignored shouts in the night. If anyone heard him, there was no sign of it, and presently Tom Benecke knew he had to try moving; there was nothing else he could do.

Eyes squeezed shut, he watched scenes in his mind like scraps of motion-picture film—he could not stop them. He saw himself stumbling suddenly sideways as he crept along the ledge and saw his upper body arc outwards, arms flailing. He saw a dangling shoestring caught between the ledge and the sole of his other shoe, saw a foot start to move, to be stopped with a jerk, and felt his balance leaving him. He saw himself falling with a terrible speed as his body revolved in the air, knees clutched tight to his chest, eyes squeezed shut, moaning softly.

Out of utter necessity, knowing that any of these thoughts might be reality in the very next seconds, he was slowly able to shut his mind against every thought but what he now began to do. With fear-soaked slowness, he slid his left foot an inch or two towards his own impossibly distant window. Then he slid the fingers of his shivering left hand a corresponding distance. For a moment he could not bring himself to lift his right foot from one ledge to the other; then he did it, and became aware of the harsh exhalation of air from his throat and realized that he was panting. As his right hand, then, began to slide along the brick edging, he was astonished to feel the yellow paper pressed to the bricks underneath his stiff fingers, and he uttered a terrible, abrupt bark that might have been a laugh or a moan. He opened his mouth and took the paper in his teeth, pulling it out from under his fingers.

By a kind of trick—by concentrating his entire mind on first his left foot, then his left hand, then the other foot, then the other hand—he was able to move, almost imperceptibly, trembling steadily, very nearly without thought. But he could feel the terrible strength of the pent-up horror on just the other side of the flimsy barrier he had erected in his mind; and he knew that if it broke through he would lose this thin, artificial control of his body.

During one slow step he tried keeping his eyes closed; it

made him feel safer, shutting him off a little from the fearful reality of where he was. Then a sudden rush of giddiness swept over him, and he had to open his eyes wide, staring sideways at the cold rough brick and angled lines of mortar, his cheek tight against the building. He kept his eyes open then, knowing that if he once let them flick outwards, to stare for an instant at the lighted windows across the street, he would be past help.

He didn't know how many dozens of tiny sidling steps he had taken, his chest, belly, and face pressed to the wall; but he knew the slender hold he was keeping on his mind and body was going to break. He had a sudden mental picture of his apartment on just the other side of this wall—warm, cheerful, incredibly spacious. And he saw himself striding through it, lying down on the floor on his back, arms spread wide, revelling in its unbelievable security. The impossible remoteness of this utter safety, the contrast between it and where he now stood, was more than he could bear. And the barrier broke then, and the fear of the awful height he stood on coursed through his nerves and muscles.

A fraction of his mind knew he was going to fall, and he began taking rapid blind steps with no feeling of what he was doing, sidling with a clumsy, desperate swiftness, fingers scrabbling along the brick, almost hopelessly resigned to the sudden backward pull and swift motion outward and down. Then his moving hand slid onto not brick but sheer emptiness, an impossible gap in the face of the wall, and he stumbled.

His right foot smashed into his left ankle bone; he staggered sideways, began falling, and the claw of his hand cracked against glass and wood, slid down it, and his finger tips were pressed hard on the puttyless edging of his window. His right hand smacked gropingly beside it as he fell to his knees; and, under the full weight and direct downward pull of his sagging body, the open window dropped shudderingly in its frame till it closed and his wrists struck the sill and were jarred off.

For a single moment he knelt, knee bones against stone on the very edge of the ledge, body swaying and touching nowhere else, fighting for balance. Then he lost it, his shoulders plunging backwards, and he flung his arms forward, his hands smashing against the window casing on either side and—his body moving backwards—his fingers clutched the narrow wood stripping of the upper pane.

For an instant he hung suspended between balance and falling, his finger tips pressed onto the quarter-inch wood strips. Then, with utmost delicacy with a focused concentration of all his senses, he increased even further the strain on his finger tips hooked to these slim edgings of wood. Elbows slowly bending, he began to draw the full weight of his upper body forward, knowing that the instant his fingers slipped off these quarter-inch strips he'd plunge backwards and be falling. Elbows imperceptibly bending, body shaking with the strain, the sweat starting from his forehead in great sudden drops, he pulled, his entire being and thought concentrated in his finger tips. Then, suddenly, the strain slackened and ended, his chest touching the window sill, and he was kneeling on the ledge, his forehead pressed to the glass of the closed window.

Dropping his palms to the sill, he stared into his living room—at the red-brown davenport across the room, and a magazine he had left there; at the pictures on the walls and the gray rug; the entrance to the hallway; and at his papers, typewriter, and desk, not two feet from his nose. A movement from his desk caught his eye, and he saw that it was a thin curl of blue smoke; his cigarette, the ash long, was still burning in the ashtray where he'd left it—this was past all belief—only a few minutes before.

His head moved, and in faint reflection from the glass before him, he saw the yellow paper clenched in his front teeth. Lifting a hand from the sill he took it from his mouth; the moistened corner parted from the paper, and he spat it out.

For a moment, in the light from the living room, he stared wonderingly at the yellow sheet in his hand and then crushed it into the side pocket of his jacket.

He couldn't open the window. It had been pulled not completely closed, but its lower edge was below the level of the outside sill; there was no room to get his fingers underneath it. Between the upper sash and the lower was a gap not wide enough—reaching up, he tried—to get his fingers into; he couldn't push it open. The upper window panel, he knew from long experience, was impossible to move, frozen tight with dried paint.

Very carefully observing his balance, the finger tips of his left hand again hooked to the narrow stripping of the window casing, he drew his right hand, palm facing the glass, and then struck the glass with the heel of his hand.

His arm rebounded from the pane, his body tottering, and he knew he didn't dare strike a harder blow.

But in the security and relief of his new position, he simply smiled; with only a sheet of glass between him and the room just before him, it was not possible that there wasn't a way past it. Eyes narrowing, he thought for a few moments about what to do. Then his eyes widened, for nothing occurred to him. But still he felt calm: the trembling, he realized, had stopped. At the back of his mind there still lay the thought that once he was again in his home, he could give release to his feelings. He actually *would* lie on the floor, rolling, clenching tufts of the rug in his hands. He would literally run across the room, free to move as he liked, jumping on the floor, testing and reveling in its absolute security, letting the relief flood through him, draining the fear from his mind and body. His yearning for this was astonishingly intense, and somehow he understood that he had better keep this feeling at bay.

He took a half dollar from his pocket and struck it against the pane, but without any hope that the glass would break and with very little disappointment when it did not. After a few moments of thought he drew his leg up on to the ledge and picked loose the knot of his shoe lace. He slipped off his shoe and, holding it across the instep, drew back his arm as far as he dared and struck the leather heel against the glass. The pane rattled, but he knew he'd been a long way from breaking it. His foot was cold and he slipped the shoe back on. He shouted again, experimentally, and then once more, but there was no answer.

The realization suddenly struck him that he might have to wait here till Clare came home, and for a moment the thought was funny. He could see Clare opening the front door, withdrawing her key from the lock, closing the door behind her, and then glancing up to see him crouched on the other side of the window. He could see her rush across the room, face astounded and frightened, and hear himself shouting instructions: "Never mind how I got here! Just open the wind——" She couldn't open it, he remembered, she'd never been able to; she'd always had to call him. She'd have to get the building superintendent or a neighbor, and he pictured himself smiling and answering their questions as he climbed in. "I just wanted to get a breath of fresh air, so—"

He couldn't possibly wait here till Clare came home. It was the second feature she'd wanted to see, and she'd left in time to see the first. She'd be another three hours or— He glanced at his watch; Clare had been gone eight minutes. It wasn't possible, but only eight minutes ago he had kissed his wife good-bye. She wasn't even in the theatre yet!

It would be four hours before she could possibly be home, and he tried to picture himself kneeling out here, finger tips hooked to these narrow strippings, while first one movie, preceded by a slow listing of credits, began, developed, reached its climax and then finally ended. There'd be a newsreel next, maybe, and then an animated cartoon, and then interminable scenes from coming pictures. And then, once more, the beginning of a full-length picture—while all the time he hung out here in the night.

He might possibly get to his feet, but he was afraid to try. Already his legs were cramped, his thigh muscles tired; his knees hurt, his feet felt numb, and his hands were stiff. He couldn't possibly stay out here for four hours or anywhere near it. Long before that his legs and arms would give out; he would be forced to try changing his position often—stiffly, clumsily, his coordination and strength gone—and he would fall. Quite realistically, he knew that he would fall; no one could stay out here on this ledge for four hours.

A dozen windows in the apartment building across the street were lighted. Looking over his shoulder, he could see the top of a man's head behind the newspaper he was reading; in another window he saw the blue-gray flicker of a television screen. No more than twenty-odd yards from his back were scores of people, and if just one of them would walk idly to his window and glance out. . . . For some moments he stared over his shoulder at the lighted rectangles, waiting. But no one appeared. The man reading his paper turned a page and then continued his reading. A figure passed another of the windows and was immediately gone.

In the inside pocket of his jacket he found a little sheaf of papers, and he pulled one out and looked at it in the light from the living room. It was an old letter, an advertisement of some sort; his name and address, in purple ink, were on a label pasted to the envelope. Gripping one end of the envelope in his teeth, he twisted it into a tight curl. From his shirt pocket he brought out a book of matches. He didn't dare let go the casing with both hands but, with the twist of paper in his teeth, he opened the match book with his free hand; then he bent one of the matches in two without tearing it from the folder, its red-tipped end now touching the striking surface. With his thumb, he rubbed the red tip across the striking area.

He did it again, then again, and still again, pressing harder each time, and the match suddenly flared, burning his thumb. But he kept it alight, cupping the match book in his hand and shielding it with his body. He held the flame to the paper in his mouth till it caught. Then he snuffed out the match flame with his thumb and forefinger careless of the burn, and replaced the book in his pocket. Taking the paper twist in his hand, he held it flame down, watching the flame crawl up the paper, till it flared bright. Then he held it behind him over the street, moving it from side to side, watching it over his shoulder, the flame flickering and guttering in the wind.

There were three letters in his pocket and he lighted each of them, holding each till the flame touched his hand and then dropping it to the street below. At one point, watching over his shoulder while the last of the letters burned, he saw the man across the street put down his paper and stand—even seeming, to Tom, to glance towards his window. But when he moved, it was only to walk across the room and disappear from sight.

There were a dozen coins in Tom Benecke's pocket and he dropped them, three or four at a time. But if they struck anyone or if anyone noticed their falling, no one connected them with their source, and no one glanced upwards.

His arms had begun to tremble from the steady strain of clinging to his narrow perch, and he did not know what to do now and was terribly frightened. Clinging to the window stripping with one hand, he again searched his pockets. But now—he had left his wallet on his dresser when he'd changed clothes—there was nothing left but the yellow sheet. It occurred to him irrelevantly that his death on the sidewalk below would be an eternal mystery; the window closed—why, how, and from where could he have fallen? No one would be able to identify his body for a time, either—the thought was somehow unbearable and increased his fear. All they'd find in his pockets would be the yellow sheet. *Contents of the dead man's pockets,* he thought, *one sheet of paper bearing pencilled notations—incomprehensible.*

He understood fully that he might actually be going to die; his arms, maintaining his balance on the ledge, were trembling steadily now. And it occurred to him then with all the force of a revelation that, if he fell, all he was ever going to have out of life he would then, abruptly, have had. Nothing, then, could ever be changed; and nothing more—no least experience or pleasure—could ever be added to his life. He wished, then, that he had not allowed his wife to go off by herself tonight—and on similar nights. He thought of all the evenings he had spent away from her, working; and he regretted them. He thought wonderingly of his fierce ambition and of the direction his life had taken; he thought of the hours he'd spent by himself, filling the yellow sheet that had brought him out here. *Contents of the dead man's pockets,* he thought with sudden fierce anger, *a wasted life.*

He was simply not going to cling here till he slipped and fell; he told himself that now. There was one last thing he could try; he had been aware of it for some moments, refusing to think about it, but now he faced it. Kneeling here on the ledge, the finger tips of one hand pressed to the narrow strip of wood, he could, he knew, draw his other hand back a yard perhaps, fist clenched tight, doing it very slowly till he sensed the outer limit of balance, then, as hard as he was able from the distance, he could drive his fist forward against the glass. If it broke, his fist smashing through, he was safe; he might cut himself badly, and probably would, but with his arm inside the room, he would be secure. But if the glass did not break, the rebound, flinging his arm back, would topple him off the ledge. He was certain of that.

He tested his plan. The fingers of his left hand claw-like on the little stripping, he drew back his other fist until his body began teetering backwards. But he had no leverage now—he could feel that there would be no force to his swing—and he moved his fist slowly forward till he rocked forward on his knees again and could sense that his swing would carry its greatest force. Glancing down, however, measuring the distance from his fist to the glass, he saw that it was less than two feet.

It occurred to him that he could raise his arm over his head, to bring it down against the glass. But, experimentally in slow motion, he knew it would be an awkward girl-like blow without the force of a driving punch, and not nearly enough to break the glass.

Facing the window, he had to drive a blow from the shoulder, he knew now, at a distance of less than two feet; and he did not know whether it would break through the heavy glass. It might; he could picture it happening, he could feel it in the nerves of his arm. And it might not; he could feel that, too—feel his fist striking this glass and being instantaneously flung back by the unbreaking pane, feel the fingers of his other hand breaking loose, nails scraping along the casing as he fell.

He waited, arm drawn back, first balled, but in no hurry to strike; this pause, he knew, might be an extension of his life. And to live even a few seconds longer, he felt, even out here on this ledge in the night, was infinitely better than to die a moment earlier than he had to. His arm grew tired, and he brought it down and rested it.

Then he knew that it was time to make the attempt. He could not kneel here hesitating indefinitely till he lost all courage to act, waiting till he slipped off the ledge. Again he drew back his arm, knowing this time that he would not bring it down till he struck. His elbow protruding over Lexington Avenue far below, the fingers of his other hand pressed down bloodlessly tight against the narrow stripping, he waited, feeling the sick tenseness and terrible excitement building. It grew and swelled towards the moment of action, his nerves tautening. He thought of Clare—just a wordless, yearning thought—and then drew his arm back just a bit more, fist so tight his fingers pained him, and knowing he was going to do it. Then with full power, with every last scrap of strength he could bring to bear, he shot his arm forward towards the glass, and he said "Clare!"

He heard the sound, felt the blow, felt himself falling forward, and his hand closed on the living-room curtains, the shards and fragments of glass showering onto the floor. And then, kneeling there on the ledge, an arm thrust into the room up to the shoulder, he began picking away the protruding slivers and great wedges of glass from the window frame, tossing them in onto the rug. And, as he grasped the edges of the empty frame and climbed into his home, he was grinning in triumph.

He did not lie down on the floor or run through the apartment, as he had promised himself; even in the first few moments it seemed to him natural and normal that he should be where he was. He simply turned to his desk, pulled the crumpled yellow sheet from his pocket and laid it down where it had been, smoothing it out; then he absently laid a pencil across it to weight it down. He shook his head, wonderingly, and turned to walk towards the closet.

There he got out his topcoat and hat and, without waiting to put them on, opened the front door and stepped out, to go and find his wife. He turned to pull the door closed and the warm air from the hall rushed through the narrow opening again. As he saw the yellow paper, the pencil flying, scooped off the desk and, unimpeded by the glassless window, sail out into the night and out of his life, Tom Benecke burst into laughter and then closed the door behind him.

The Warlock

FRITZ LEIBER

There was something feverish and distorted and unreal about the interest we all took in art and in Jamie.

Today witch-hunting is an unpopular occupation. Unless the witch happens to be a Red, the hunter gets a very bad Press. Just the same, today as in the Middle Ages, when a decent man recognizes a real witch—the modern equivalent of a witch by the best scientific standards—then he must instantly strike down the monster for the sake of the community without counting the cost to himself.

That is why I killed my friend Jamie Bingham Walsh, the portrait painter and interior designer. He didn't commit suicide, nor did he accidentally tumble off the scenic high point of the Latigo Canyon Road in the Santa Monica Mountains. I pushed him off with my little MG.

Oh, the car never touched him, though it very well might have—that was one of the necessary chances I took. But in the end he reacted just as I'd been banking on it that he would—in a senseless panic, avoiding the closest threat to himself, the closest pain.

I stopped the car an exact dozen feet from the verge and he got out and walked around in front to the very edge, to take one of those God-like looks at things below that he always had to take. He remarked, "The old sculptor poked his finger pretty deep here into the stone, didn't he?" Then, as he was staring down at the twisting hazy valley and the lesser hilltops crowned with brown rocks like robed monsters, I silently eased the stick into low gear. Then I softly called his name and as he turned I smiled at him and gunned the car forward an exact dozen feet, thinking of my sister Alice and looking straight at his damned green necktie. I was very precise about it. Two inches more and my front wheels would have been over the edge.

He could have frozen, in which case I'd have knocked him off, and he'd have been found with some extra injuries that might have been difficult to explain, or all too easy. Or, if he had reacted instantly, he could have jumped out of the way to either side or even onto the hood of the car—a man as much of a romantic daredevil as Jamie *looked* might have done just that, taking his chance that I didn't intend going over with him.

But he did none of those things. Instead he sprang backwards, into the great soft sweep of space above the toy valley, away from the nearest hurt. As he did so, as his nerve cracked under that final testing, it seemed to me that he instantly lost all his black power over me, so that it was a cardboard man, a phantom, who stared wildly at me for an instant from the floorless air across the creamy hood of the MG before gravity snatched him out of sight.

The mind is a funny thing and has curious self-willed blind spots. Mine was so full of the thought that I had destroyed Jamie *utterly* that it never registered at all the thud of his body hitting, though I distinctly heard the distant tinkle of a couple of pebbles as they bounced against the bulges of the rocky wall on their way down.

I sat there calm and cold, thinking of Jamie's two wives and my sister Alice and the five other women I knew about and the half-dozen of his close male friends and all his other victims whose names I would never know. I wonder if they'd have given me a round of applause from their various state mental hospitals and private sanatoriums if I'd been able to tell them I had just avenged them on the man who sent them there. I couldn't answer that question—some people always love their destroyer—but I knew that now at least there wouldn't be any more unfortunates going to join them and they wouldn't have to endure any more kindly useless visits from Jamie with his vivid neckties and his patter about a person's color. That necktie jazz, you know, was one of the first things that put me on to Jamie—I remembered that he'd told Alice that green was "her color" and then he'd worn a green necktie when he went to visit her at the asylum. Later I noticed the same tie-in (ha!) with others of his victims, except the color would be different in each case. Everybody had a color, according to Jamie—something to do with what he called the atmosphere of your mind. Mine, I now remembered he'd often told me, was blue. Blue, like the cloudless sky over Latigo.

I shivered and smiled and wiped the cold sweat off my forehead and then I backed up my MG and drove off down the canyon. That was the end of it. I never had to exchange a single word with the police. I simply wasn't connected with the affair.

And so Jamie Walsh departed from this life without putting

up any resistance whatever. He went away from us like the man who follows the usher without asking any questions when the light tap comes on his shoulder.

But perhaps Jamie didn't expect any attack. Perhaps he never knew how blackly evil he was. Perhaps he never realized he was a witch. This is a possibility I must face.

To me a witch—a modern witch, a *real* witch—is a person who is *a carrier of insanity,* one who infects others with this or that deadly psychosis without showing any of the symptoms himself, one who may be brilliantly sane by all psychiatric tests but who nevertheless carries in his mind-stream the germs of madness.

It's obviously true when you think it over. Medical science recognizes that there are such carriers of physical disease—outwardly untainted persons who spread the germs of TB, say, or typhoid fever. They're immune, they have built up a resistance, but most of those with whom they come in contact are defenseless. Typhoid Mary was a famous instance—a cook who over and over again infected hundreds of people.

By the same reasoning, Jamie Bingham Walsh should have been known as Schizo Jimmie. People with whom he came in really close contact had their minds split and started to live in dream worlds. I secretly thought of him as Schizo Jimmie for years before I gained the courage and complete certainty that let me wipe him out. The immune carrier of insanity is just as real a scientific phenomenon as the immune carrier of tuberculosis.

Most of us are willing to recognize the carrier of insanity when he operates at the national or international level. No one would deny that Hitler was such a carrier, spreading madness among his followers until he grew so powerful that there was no asylum strong enough to hold him. Lenin was a subtler and therefore better example, a seemingly sane man whose madness appeared full-grown only among his successors. And there was surely such a carrier abroad at the time of the American Civil War, there was so much madness then in high places—but I believe I have made my point.

While we generally agree on these top-of-the-heap historic cases, many of us refuse to recognize that there are Schizo Jimmies and Manic Marys and Paranoid Petes operating at all levels of society, including our own. But just think a minute about your friends and relatives and acquaintances. Don't you know at least one person who seems to be a focus for trouble without being an obvious troublemaker? A jinxy sort of guy or gal whose close friends show a remarkable tendency to crack up, to suicide perhaps, to call the headshrinkers a bit too late, to take long vacations in the looney bin—or vacations that are longer than long. More likely than not he's brilliant and charming and seems to have the best intentions in the world (Jamie Walsh was all those things and more), but he's just not good for people.

At first you think he's merely unlucky in his choice of friends and maybe you feel sorry for him, and then you begin to wonder if he doesn't have a special talent or compulsion for seeking out and taking up with unstable people, and finally, if circumstances force you as deep into the thing as they did me, you begin to suspect that there's more to it than that. A lot more.

Alice and I got to know Jamie Walsh when Father hired him to do an interior design job on our new home in Malibu and also, it had already been arranged two days later, to paint Mother with the Afghan hounds. Jamie was in his late thirties then, energetic as hell, a real cosmopolite, impudent, flamingly charming, and he hit our soberly intelligent household like a whirlwind. He was a terrific salesman, as you have to be in that sort of job, and everyone in the vicinity got an absolutely painless bonus course in general culture—Modigliani, Swedish Modern, the works.

With the price he was getting, we certainly had a bonus coming, but we didn't think about it that way. He'd come in, waving a devil mask, or a sari, or a hunk of period wrought iron or a gaudy old chamberpot, and the day's show would be on. For three months he was a non-resident member of the family. It was exactly like being visited by a pleasantly wicked young uncle you've never seen before because he's been completely occupied having exciting adventures in strange corners of the world and also, quite incidentally, happens to be a genius.

Within two weeks Jamie was painting Alice and myself as a matter of course and in the end he even sculptured a head of Father—cast in aluminum for some abstruse reason—and that was something I'd have given odds against ever happening. But in the end, as I say, even Father was bit by the art bug and for perhaps a month his old airplane factory took second place in his interests—the only time I'm sure, before or since, that ever happened in Father's life.

There was something feverish and distorted and unreal about the interest we all took in art and in Jamie at that time. He was like a hypnotist or some master magician weaving spells, creating wonderful dream worlds.

I dropped my forced interest in Father's business and my vaguer secret ambitions to do something in psychiatry, and determined to devote my life to marine painting, at which I'd earlier shown some talent. I let the others think it was a passing kick, which made things easier, especially with Father, but it was a lot more than that.

As for Alice, she seemed on the surface to be the least affected of all of us—she didn't sprout an artistic talent—but really she was the hardest hit. For she fell in love with Jamie. And he, in his peculiar way, encouraged her.

It wasn't anything obvious, mind you. I'm sure I was the only other person who realized what was happening, and at the time I didn't care. In fact it seemed to me to be a fine thing that I should be able to offer up a beautiful sister to Jamie and that he should be interested. Since then I've noticed that many men have the urge, usually unconscious—or so they'd claim—to furnish the services of their wives, sisters, and daughters to friends. It seems to be about as common as the opposite urge to clobber any male who so much as looks at their womenfolk, and is probably equally primitive in origin.

Mother may have guessed that Alice had developed a crush on Jamie, but I'm sure that was as far as her guesses went. She was herself too much under Jamie's spell to think unsympathetically of him. You see, by this time we'd learned about Jamie's unhappy marriage—he'd tried, or seemed to try, to conceal it, but it had come out all the same—how his wife Jane was a hopeless alcoholic who spent most of her time touring the sanatoriums and that one reason Jamie had to work so furiously was to pay the bills. Even I didn't dream at the time that Jane was just another of his victims and that what kept her alcoholism flaring was his ambiguous behavior towards her—his wanting her and not wanting her at the same time, his simultaneous caring for her and getting rid of her via the asylum route. She'd caught the infection he carried and in her case it was alcohol that was nursing the infection along.

But at the time even I knew nothing of this, and we were all sympathy for Jamie and his troubles, we were all living in his bright dream worlds. Alice, I'm certain, was existing for the day when Jamie would carry her off—to marriage or a fierce selfish love-affair, I don't imagine she cared which. Just as I didn't care, deep in my old subconscious, whether I became a famous marine painter or merely Jamie's assistant. Alice and I were both of us building up to a big thing happening.

What happened was exactly nothing. Jamie finished the jobs Father had hired him to do and took off for Mexico all by himself. Mother went back to playing bridge. I threw my paint boxes into the ocean I'd been trying to catch on canvas. And Alice flipped, signalizing the event by shooting the two Afghan hounds.

Mother and Father were stunned, of course, but they still didn't connect up the tragedy in any way with Jamie. And I must admit that, if you didn't want to dig, there were enough old reasons around for Alice flipping—she'd always been a shy, difficult child with a mass of personality problems, she'd a terrific problem fighting overweight, later she'd dropped out of college twice, dithered around with different career dreams, been mixed up with some kids who were on dope, and so on.

No, I was the only one who saw the real part that Jamie played in the business. Mother and Father actually took the attitude that Jamie had been a *good* influence on Alice, that she'd have flipped sooner if it hadn't been for his stimulating presence and the general air of activity and excitement he brought into our otherwise stolid lives. In fact they took this attitude so deeply that when Jamie came bustling back from Venezuela six months later, all shocked sympathy at Alice's tragedy but at the same time yarning of his new adventures—he had a jaguar skin for Mother—they fell in eagerly with his idea of visiting Alice at the mental hospital. They thought it might have a good effect on her, wake her up and all that.

And I was the one who had to drive him there. I, who had begun to shrink from him because I sensed that he was dripping—honestly, that's the way it felt to me—with the invisible germs of madness. I, who remembered how he'd told Alice that green was "her color" and realized now the significance of the green necktie he was wearing.

I don't know, mind you, if *he* realized its significance. All through this, as I've said, I've been uncertain of the degree to which Jamie realized that he was creating the tragedies around him, the extent to which he knew that he was a carrier.

It was a long lonely drive under cloudless skies, prefiguring in a way the final drive I took with Jamie. As we had got in the car he had looked up at the sky and recalled that blue was *my* color. It gave me the shudders, but I didn't let on. I remember thinking, though, of the odd sensitivities painters are supposed to have. Sargent once painted a woman, and a doctor who'd never met her diagnosed incipient insanity from the portrait, and the diagnosis was confirmed shortly.

Then after a bit Jamie fell into an odd wistful mood of faintly humorous self-pity and he told me about the dismal end his wife had come to in a New York hospital and about the numbers of his close friends who had flipped or suicided.

I'm sure he didn't realize that he was giving me research materials that were to occupy my real thinking for the next several years.

At the same time I began to see in a shadowy way the mechanism by which Jamie operated as a carrier of insanity—something I understand very well now.

You see, there has to be a mechanism, or else this transmission of insanity I'm talking about would be nothing but witchcraft—just as the transmission of physical disease was once thought by most people to be a matter of witchcraft.

Then the microscope came and germs were discovered to be the cause of infectious disease.

What causes insanity, at least the schizoid kind, what

transmits it and carries it, is *dreams*—waking dreams, daytime dreams, the most powerful and virulent of all.

Jamie awakened and fostered dreams of romance in every woman he met. They looked at him, they listened to him, they lost themselves in the golden dream of a love affair that would dazzle the ages. And then . . . Jamie did nothing at all about it. Nothing brave, nothing reckless, not even anything cruel or merely male-hungry. Like the others, Jamie just left Alice hanging there.

In men it was dreams of glory that Jamie roused, dreams of adventures and artistic achievements quite beyond their real capabilities. It was their jobs that the men abandoned—their schooling, their common sense. Just as it happened to me, except that I saw Jamie's trap in time and threw my paints away.

But in one sense I was trapped more completely by Jamie than any of the others, because it was given to me to sense the menace of the man and to realize that I must study this thing and then do something about it, no matter how long it took or how much it hurt me.

Yes, I became aware of all those things in a shadowy way on that first drive from Malibu to the mental hospital—and I also got one piece of very concrete evidence against Jamie, though it was years before I realized its full significance.

After Jamie tired of talking he closed his eyes and went into a sort of uneasy drowse beside me. After a while he twisted on his narrow seat and he began to mutter and murmur in a rhythmic way as if, half asleep, he were making up or repeating a jingle to the spin of the wheels and the buzz of the motor. I still don't know what sort of mental process in Jamie was responsible for it—creativity takes strange twists. I listened carefully and after a while I began to catch words and then more words. He kept repeating the same thing. These are the words I caught:

Beth is sand-brown, Brenda's gray,
Dottie was mauve and faded away.
Hans was scarlet, Dave was black,
Keith was cobalt and off the track.

Ridiculous words. And then I thought, "I'm blue."

Jamie woke up and asked what had been happening. "Nothing," I told him and that seemed to satisfy him. We were practically at the asylum.

Jamie's visit to Alice was no help to her that I could see—on her next trip home she was just as out of touch and even more disgustingly fat—but that was how I became Jamie's Boswell, interested in every person he'd known, every place he'd been, anything he'd ever done or said. I talked with him a lot and with his friends more. One way or another, I managed to visit most of the places he'd been. Father was alternately furious and depressed at the way I was "wasting my life." He'd have tried to stop me, except that what had happened to Alice had put the fear into him of tampering with his children. We were queer eggs and might crack and smell. Of course he hadn't the faintest idea of what I was doing. I don't think that even Jamie guessed. Jamie responded to my interest with half-amused tolerance, though from time to time I caught an odd look in his eyes.

In the course of five years I accumulated enough evidence to convict James Bingham Walsh a dozen times of being a carrier of insanity. I found out about his younger brother, who had hero-worshipped him, tried to imitate him, done a bad job of it and abberrated before he was twenty . . . about his first wife, who'd only managed to stay a year this side of the asylum walls . . . about Hans Godbold, who ditched his family and an executive job in a big chemical firm to become a poet and who six months later blew out his brains in Panama. About David Willis, Keith Ellander, Elizabeth Hunter, Brenda Silverstein, Dorothy Williamson . . . "colored people—scarlet, black, cobalt, sand-brown, gray, mauve"—for now I remembered the jingle he'd muttered in my ear. . . .

It wasn't just a matter of individuals. Statistics contributed their quota. Wherever Jamie went, if it was a small enough place for it to show up and if I could get the figures, there was a rise, small but undeniable, in the incidence of insanity. Make no mistake, Jamie Bingham Walsh deserved the name of Schizo Jimmie.

And then, as I've told you, when my evidence was complete, when it wholly satisfied *me,* I acted. I was prosecutor, judge, jury, and executioner all rolled into one. Sometimes when you're a little ahead of the science of your day, it has to be that way. I marched the prisoner up Latigo Canyon—by chance wearing a green tie, Alice's color, which made me happy—and he made the big drop.

The only thing that really bothers me about it all now is my unshaken conviction that Jamie was a genius. A master manipulator of colors, and whether he knew it or not, of people. It is too bad that he was too dangerous to be let live. I sometimes think that the same is true of all so-called "great men"—they create dreams that infect and rot or crumble the minds of the rest of us. They are carriers, even the most seemingly noble and compassionate of them. At the time of the American Civil War the chief carrier was that sufferer from involutional melancholia, that tormented man from whom knives once had to be hidden, Abraham Lincoln. Oh, why can't such men leave us little people to our own kinds of safety and happiness, our small plans and small successes, our security firmly based on our mediocrity? Why must they keep spreading the deadly big dreams?

Naturally enough, I haven't escaped from this affair scot-free, though as I've told you I've been in no trouble with the police or the law. But just the same it was too tough a job for one man, too much responsibility for one person to shoulder. It left its mark on me, all right. By the time I'd finished, my nerves were like crackle glass. That's why I'm in this . . . well . . . rest home now, why I may be here for a long time. I concentrated so much on the one big problem that when it was solved I just couldn't seem to attend to life any more.

I'm not asking for pity, understand. I did what I had to, I did what any decent man would do, and I'm glad I was brave enough. I'm not complaining about any of the consequences I'm suffering now, the inevitable consequences of my frazzled nerves. I don't care if I have to spend the rest of my life here—I'm not complaining about the dreams . . . the mental hurting . . . the flow of ideas too fast for thought or comment . . . the voices I hear . . . the hallucinations. . . .

Except that I *am* bothered, I admit, by the hallucinations I have of Jamie coming to visit me here. They are so real that some days they make me wonder whether they aren't the real live Jamie and whether it wasn't just the hallucination of Jamie that I sent hurtling down to his death in Latigo Canyon. After all, he never said a word, he looked like a phantom hanging in the air, and I never heard the sound of his body hitting.

Those are the days when I wish the police *would* come and question me about his death—question me, try me, condemn me, and send me to the gas chamber and out of this life that is no more than a torrent of tortured dreams. The days when Jamie comes to visit me, smiling tenderly and wearing a blue necktie.

The Pipe-Smoker

MARTIN ARMSTRONG

There were five faces—all supposed to be identical: but the fifth one was the cause of great consternation.

I don't usually mind walking in the rain, but on this occasion the rain was coming down in torrents and I had still ten miles to go. That was why I stopped at the first house, a house about a mile from the village ahead of me, and looked over the garden gate. The house didn't look promising, for I saw at once that it was empty. All the windows were shut, and not one of them had a blind or a curtain. Through one on the ground floor I saw bare walls, a bare mantelpiece, and an empty grate. The garden too was wild, the beds full of weeds; you would hardly have known it for a garden but for the fence, the vestiges of straight paths, and the lilac bushes which were in full bloom and sent showers of water to the grass every time the wind tossed them.

You can imagine, then, that I was surprised when a man strolled out from the lilacs and came slowly toward me down the path. What was surprising was not merely that he was there, but that he was strolling aimlessly about, bareheaded and without a mackintosh, in the drenching rain. He was rather a fat man and dressed like a clergyman, gray-haired, bald, clean-shaven, with that swollen-headed and over-intense look which one sees in portraits of William Blake. I noticed at once how his arms hung limply at his sides. His clothes and—what made him still stranger—his face were streaming with water! He didn't seem to be in the least aware of the rain. But I was. It was beginning to trickle through my hair and down my neck, and I said:

"Excuse me, sir, but may I come in and shelter?"

He started and raised puzzled eyes to mine. "Shelter?" he said.

"Yes," I replied, "from the rain."

"Ah, from the rain. Yes, sir, by all means. Pray come in."

I opened the garden gate and followed him down a path toward the front door, where he stood aside with a slight bow to let me pass in first. "I fear you won't find it very comfortable," he said when we were in the hall. "However, come in, sir; in here, first door on the left."

The room, which was a large one with a bow window divided into five lights, was empty, except for a deal table and bench and a smaller table in a corner near the door with an unlighted lamp on it.

"Pray sit down, sir," he said, pointing to the bench with another slight bow. There was an old-fashioned politeness in his manner and language. He himself did not sit down, but walked to the window and stood looking out at the streaming garden, his arms still hanging idly at his sides.

"Apparently you don't mind rain as much as I do, sir," I said, in an attempt to be amiable.

He turned around, and I had the impression that he could not turn his head and so had to turn his whole body in order to look at me. "No, no, no!" he replied. "Not at all. In point of fact, I hadn't observed it until you pointed it out."

"But you must be very wet," I said. "Wouldn't it be wiser to change?"

"To change?" His gaze became searching and suspicious at the question.

"To change your wet clothes."

"Change my clothes?" he said. "Oh, no! Oh, dear me, no, sir! If they're wet, doubtless they'll dry in course of time. It isn't raining in here, I take it?"

I looked at his face. He really was asking for information. "No," I replied, "it isn't raining in here, thank goodness."

"I fear I can't offer you anything," he said politely. "A woman comes from the village in the morning and evening, but meanwhile I'm quite helpless." He opened and closed his hanging hands. "Unless," he added, "you would care to go to the kitchen and make yourself a cup of tea, if you understand such things."

I refused, but asked leave to smoke a cigarette.

"Pray do," he said. "I fear I have none to offer you. The other, my predecessor, used to smoke cigarettes, but I'm a pipe-smoker." He brought a pipe and pouch from his pocket: it was a relief to see him use his arms and hands.

When we had both lit up, I spoke again: I was conscious all the while that the responsibility for conversation was mine; that, if I had not spoken, my strange host would have made no attempt to break the silence, but would have stood with his

arms at his sides looking straight in front of him e
garden or at me.

I glanced around the bare room. "You're just
suppose?" I said.

"Moving in?" He shifted slightly and turned
uncomfortable gaze on me again.

"Moving into this house, I mean."

"Oh, no," he said. "Oh, dear me, no, sir. I've
several years; or rather, I myself have been her
year, and the other, my predecessor, was here
before that. Yes, it must be seven months now s
away. No doubt, sir"—a melancholy, wistful s
edly transformed his face—"no doubt you
me—Mrs. Bellows wouldn't—when I tell you
only seven months, there or thereabouts."

"If you say so, sir," I replied, "why sho
you?"

He took a few steps toward me and liftec
Reluctantly I took it, a thick, limp, cold hanc
unpleasant thrill. "Thank you, sir," he s
You're the first, absolutely the first—!"

I dropped the hand and he did not finish t
fallen, apparently, into a reverie. Then he
doubt all would have been well if only
predecessor's old cousin had not left him
better off where he was. He was a clergym
opened his hands, exhibiting himself. "The

Again he absented himself, fell into a re
in its clergyman's clothes stood before me
me, "Do you believe in confession?"

"In confession?" I said. "You mean in
the term?"

He took a step closer. He was almo

"What I mean is," he said, lowering his voice and looking at me intensely, "do you believe that to confess a sin or a—a crime, brings relief?"

What was he going to tell me? I should have liked to say no, to discourage any confession from the poor old creature, but he had put his question so appealingly that I could not find it in ny heart to repulse him. "Yes," I said, "I think that by peaking of it one can often rid oneself of a weight on the nind."

"You have been so sympathetic, sir," he said with one of his olite bows, "that I feel tempted to trespass—!" He lifted one f his heavy hands in a perfunctory gesture and dropped it gain. "Would you have the patience to listen?"

He stood beside me as if he had been a tailor's dummy that ad been placed there. His leg touched my knee. I felt strongly pelled by his closeness. "Won't you sit down there?" I said, inting to the other end of the bench on which I was sitting. "I ould find it easier to listen."

He turned his body and gazed earnestly at the bench, then down on it, facing me, a leg on either side of it, leaning ward me. He was about to speak, but he checked himself and nced at the window and the door. Then he took his pipe m his mouth and laid it on the table, and his eyes returned to . "My secret, my terrible secret," he said, "is that I'm a rderer."

His statement horrified me, as well it might; and yet, I think, ardly surprised me. His extreme strangeness had prepared to some extent, for something rather grim. I caught my ath and stared at him, and he, with horror in his eyes, stared k at me. He seemed to be waiting for me to speak, but at I could not speak. What, in the name of sanity, could I What I did say was something fantastically inadequate. d this," I said, "weighs on your mind?"

"It haunts me," he said, suddenly clenching his heavy, limp hands that lay on the bench in front of him. "Would you have the patience—?"

I nodded. "Tell me about it," I said.

"If it hadn't been for the legacy of this house," he began, "nothing would have happened. The other, my predecessor, would have stayed in his rectory, and I—I should never have come on the scene at all. Although it must be confessed that he, my predecessor, was not happy in his rectory. He met with unfriendliness, suspicion. That was why he first came to this house—just as a trial, you see. It was bequeathed to him empty: simply the house—no furniture, no money—and he came and put in one or two things—this table, this bench, a few kitchen things, a folding bed upstairs. He wanted, you see, to try it, first. Its remoteness appealed to him, but he wanted to be sure about it in other ways. Some houses, you see, are safe, and some are not, and he wanted to make sure that this was a safe house before moving into it." He paused and then said very earnestly, "Let me advise you, my friend, always to do that when you contemplate moving into a strange house—because some houses are very unsafe."

I nodded. "Quite so!" I said. "Damp walls, bad drainage, and so on."

He shook his head. "No," he said, "not that. Something much more serious than that. I mean the spirit of the house. Don't you feel"—his gaze grew more piercing than ever—"that this is a dangerous house?"

I shrugged my shoulders. "Empty houses are always a little queer," I said.

He reflected on this statement. "And you have noticed," he inquired at last, "the queerness of this one?"

I did, as he asked me the question, feel that the house was queer; but it was *his* queerness, I knew well enough, and the grim suggestiveness of his talk, that made it so, and I replied, "Not queerer than other empty houses, sir."

He gazed at me incredulously. "Strange!" he said. "Strange that you shouldn't feel it. Though it's true that—that the other, my predecessor, didn't feel it at first. Even this room—for this room, sir, is the dangerous room—didn't seem strange to him at first; no, even in spite of a very peculiar thing about it."

If it had been fine weather, I should have ended the conversation and left him, for the old man's talk and manner were making me feel more and more uncomfortable. But it was not fine: it was raining as hard as ever and was becoming very dark. Evidently we were in for a thunderstorm.

The old man got up from the bench. "I think I can show you, now," he said, "the peculiar thing about the room. It is visible only after dark, but I think it is dark enough now."

He went to the little table in the corner and began to light the lamp. When it was alight and he had replaced the frosted glass globe, he brought it to the larger table and set it down to my left. "Now," he said, "sit square to the table."

I did so. Before me across the bare room was the curtainless five-lighted bow window.

"You are sitting now," he said, laying a heavy hand on my shoulder, "where the other, my predecessor, used to sit and take his meals."

I could not restrain a start, nor resist the impulse to turn and face him. It made me uneasy to have him standing over me, behind me, out of sight. He appeared surprised. "Pray don't be alarmed, sir," he said, "but turn back and tell me what you see."

I obeyed. "I see the window," I said.

"Is that all?" he asked.

I stared at the window. "No," I said. "I also see five reflections of myself, one in each light of the window."

"Just so," said the old man, "just so! That is what the other saw when he took his meals alone. He saw the five other selves each eating its lonely meal. When he poured out some water, each of them poured out water: when he lit a cigarette, each of them lit a cigarette."

"Of course," I said. "And that alarmed your friend, the clergyman?"

"The Reverend James Baxter," said the old man; "that was his name. Be sure not to forget it, my friend; and if people ask you who lives here, remember to say the Reverend James Baxter. Nobody knows, you see, that—that—!"

"Nobody knows what you told me. I understand."

"Exactly!" he said, suddenly dropping his voice. "Nobody knows. Not a soul. You're the first person I've mentioned it to."

"And you've had no inquiries?" I asked. "This Mr. Baxter was not missed?"

He shook his head. "No," he said. "Even Mrs. Bellows, who looked after him from the start, is not aware of what happened."

I turned around and faced him incredulously. "Not aware, you mean to say—"

"Not aware that I'm not he. You see," he explained, "we were very much alike. Quite remarkably so! I can show you a photograph of him before you go and you'll see for yourself."

I now decided that, rain or no rain, I would go; there did not seem much reason, beyond the rain, for my staying. I stood up. "Well, sir," I said, "I can only hope that you will feel the benefit of having relieved your mind of your—secret."

The old gentleman became very much agitated. He clasped and unclasped his two limp hands. "Oh, but you must not go yet. You haven't heard half of it. You haven't heard how it happened. I had hoped, sir—you have been so kind—that you'd have the patience and the kindness to—!"

I sat down again on the bench. "By all means," I said, "if you have more to say."

"I had just told you, hadn't I," the old gentleman went on, "that I—that the other—that my predecessor used to sit here at his meals and see his five other selves mimicking him? When he lit his cigarette he saw five other cigarettes lighted simultaneously—!"

"Naturally," I said.

"Yes, naturally," said the old boy; "it was all perfectly natural, as you say; perfectly natural until one night, one terrible night." He stopped and stared at me with horror in his eyes.

"And then?" I said.

"Then a strange, a dreadful thing happened. When he, my predecessor, had lit his cigarette, watching those other selves, as he always did, he saw that one of them, the one on the extreme left, had lit, not a cigarette, but a pipe."

I burst out laughing. "Oh, come, come, sir!"

The old man wrung his hands in agitation. "It is comic, I know," he said, "but it is also terrible. What would you have thought if you had actually *seen* it yourself? Wouldn't you have been appalled?"

"Yes," I said, "if it had actually happened. If I had really seen such a thing, of course I should."

"Well," said the old fellow, "it *did* happen. There was no possible mistake about it. It was appalling, ghastly." There was as much horror in his voice as if he had actually seen the thing himself.

"But, my dear sir," I said to him, "you have only the word of this Mr.—Mr. Baxter for it."

He stared at me, his eyes blazing with conviction. "I *know* it happened," he said; "I know it much more certainly than if I had seen it. Listen. The thing went on for five days: on five successive evenings my predecessor watched in horror for the thing to right itself."

"But why didn't he go—leave the house?" I asked.

"He daren't go," said the old man in a strained whisper. "He daren't go: he *had* to stay and see for certain that the thing had righted itself."

"And it didn't?"

"On the sixth night," said the old man with bated breath, "the fifth reflection, the one that had broken away from obedience, had gone."

"Gone?"

"Yes, gone from the window. My predecessor sat gazing in terror at the blank pane and the other four stared back in terror into this room. He glanced from the empty pane to them and they stared back at him, or at something behind him, with horror in their eyes. Then he began to choke—to choke," gasped the old man, himself almost choking, "to choke, because hands were around his throat, clutching, throttling him."

"You mean that the hands were the hands of the fifth?" I asked, and it was only my horror at the old man's horror that prevented my smiling cynically.

"Yes," he hissed, and he held out his thick, heavy hands, gazing at me with staring eyes. "Yes. *My* hands!"

For the first time I was really terrified. We stared speechless at one another, he still gasping and wheezing. Then, hoping to soothe him, I said as calmly as I could, "I see. So *you* were the fifth reflection?"

He pointed to his pipe on the table. "Yes," he gasped; "I, the pipe-smoker."

I stood up. My impulse was to hurry to the door. But some

scruple held me there still, a feeling that it would be inhuman to leave him alone, a prey to his horrible fantasy; and, with a vague idea of bringing him to his senses, of easing his tortured mind, I asked, "And what did you do with the body?"

He caught his breath, a shudder distorted his face, and, clenching his two extended hands, he began to beat his breast convulsively. "*This,* " he shouted in a voice of agony, "*this* is the body."